The
BREAKING
OF THE OUTER MAN
AND THE RELEASE OF THE

SPIRIT

WATCHMAN NEE

Living Stream Ministry
Anaheim, California • www.lsm.org

First Edition, June 1997.

ISBN 1-57593-955-X

Published by

Living Stream Ministry
2431 W. La Palma Ave., Anaheim, CA 92801 U.S.A.
P. O. Box 2121, Anaheim, CA 92814 U.S.A.

Printed in the United States of America

04 05 06 07 / 13 12 11 10 9 8 7 6

CONTENTS

PREFACE

This book discusses a fundamental lesson facing a servant of Christ—the breaking of the outer man by the Lord for the release of the spirit. The only work God approves is that of the spirit, and the breaking of the outer man is the only way that the spirit can have full freedom.

All of these messages were given by Watchman Nee during his training in Kuling for his co-workers in 1948 and 1949. May the Lord bless the readers through these pages.

CHAPTER ONE

THE IMPORTANCE OF BREAKING

Scripture Reading: John 12:24; Heb. 4:12-13; 1 Cor. 2:11-14; 2 Cor. 3:6; Rom. 1:9; 7:6; 8:4-8; Gal. 5:16, 22-23, 25

Sooner or later a servant of God discovers that he himself is the greatest frustration to his work. Sooner or later he finds that his outer man does not match his inner man. The inner man heads in one direction, while the outer man heads in another direction. He discovers that his outer man cannot be subject to the rule of the spirit and cannot walk according to God's highest demands. He discovers that the greatest hindrance to his work is his outer man and that this outer man frustrates him from exercising his spirit. Every servant of God should be able to exercise his spirit, to secure God's presence in his spirit, to know God's word through his spirit, to touch men's condition by his spirit, to convey God's word through his spirit, and to sense and receive divine revelation with his spirit. Yet the frustration of the outer man makes it impossible for him to use his spirit. Many servants of the Lord are fundamentally unfit for the Lord's work because they have never been dealt with by the Lord in a fundamental way. Without this dealing, they are basically unqualified for any work. All excitement, zeal, and earnest pleading is vain. This kind of fundamental dealing is the only way for us to become a useful vessel to the Lord.

THE OUTER MAN AND THE INNER MAN

Romans 7:22 says, "For I delight in the law of God according to the inner man." Our inner man delights in the law of God. Ephesians 3:16 also tells us "to be strengthened with power through His Spirit into the inner man." In 2 Corinthians 4:16 Paul also said, "Though our outer man is

decaying, yet our inner man is being renewed day by day."
The Bible divides our being into the outer man and the inner
man. God resides in the inner man, and the man outside this
God-occupied inner man is the outer man. In other words, our
spirit is the inner man, while the person that others contact
is the outer man. Our inner man puts on our outer man like a
garment. God has placed Himself, His Spirit, His life, and His
power in us, that is, in our inner man. Outside of our inner
man is our mind, emotion, and will. Outside of all these is our
body, our flesh.

In order for a man to work for God, his inner man must be
released. The fundamental problem with many servants of
God is that their inner man cannot break out of their outer
man. In order for the inner man to be released, it must break
out of the outer man. We have to be clear that the first obstacle to our work is ourselves, not other things. If our inner man
is an imprisoned, confined man, our spirit is shrouded and
not easily released. If we have never learned to break through
our outer man with our spirit, we cannot work for the Lord.
Nothing frustrates us like the outer man. Whether or not our
work will be effective depends on whether the Lord has
broken down our outer man and whether the inner man can
be released through our broken, outer man. This is a very
fundamental issue. The Lord has to dismantle our outer man
in order to make way for our inner man. As soon as the inner
man is released, many sinners will be blessed and many
Christians will receive grace.

DEATH AND THE BEARING OF FRUIT

In John 12:24 the Lord Jesus said, "Unless the grain of
wheat falls into the ground and dies, it abides alone; but if it
dies, it bears much fruit." Life is in the grain. However, there
is a shell outside of the grain, a very powerful shell. As long
as this shell does not break open, the grain cannot grow.
"Unless the grain of wheat falls into the ground and dies."
What is this death? It is the action of the temperature and
moisture of the earth upon the grain which results in the
breaking of the shell. When the shell breaks, the grain grows.
Therefore, it is not a matter of whether or not the grain has

life, but whether the outer shell is broken. The very next verse says, "He who loves his soul-life loses it; and he who hates his soul-life in this world shall keep it unto eternal life" (v. 25). According to the Lord the outer shell is our own life, and the inner life is the eternal life that He dispenses. In order for the inner life to be released, the outer life must suffer loss. If that which is outward is not broken, that which is inward cannot be released.

Among all the people in the world, some have the Lord's life within them. Among those who have the Lord's life, we find two different kinds of conditions. With the first, the life is bound, surrounded, and locked up. With the second, the Lord has opened up a way and the life can be released. The problem with us today is not how we can have life, but how we can allow this life to flow out of us. When we say that the Lord has to break us, this is not a figure of speech or a doctrine. Our very being has to be broken by the Lord. The Lord's life is well able to spread over the whole earth. However, it is locked up within us! The Lord is well able to bless the church, yet His life is imprisoned, contained, and blocked in us! If the outer man is not broken, we can never become a blessing to the church, nor can we expect the world to receive God's grace through us!

THE NEED FOR THE BREAKING
OF THE ALABASTER FLASK

The Bible speaks of ointment of pure nard (John 12:3). God's Word purposely uses the adjective *pure*. It is ointment of pure nard, something truly spiritual. Unless the alabaster flask is broken, however, the ointment of pure nard cannot be released. It is strange that many people appreciate the alabaster flask. They think that the flask is more precious than the ointment. Many people think that their outer man is more precious than their inner man. This is the problem facing the church today. We may treasure our own wisdom and think that we are quite superior. Another person may treasure his emotions and also think that he is quite outstanding. Many people treasure themselves; they think that they are much better than others. They think their eloquence, their ability, their discernment, and their judgment are better. But we are not antique collectors; we are not admirers of alabaster flasks. We are those who are after the aroma of the ointment. If the outer part is not broken, the inner part will not be released. We will have no way to go on, and the church will have no way to go on. We no longer should be so protective of ourselves.

The Holy Spirit has never stopped working. Many people can testify that this work has never stopped in them. They face one trial after another, encounter one incident after another. The Holy Spirit has only one goal in all of His disciplining work: To break and dismantle the outer man so that the inner man can break forth. But the trouble with us is that we murmur as soon as we suffer a little hardship, and we complain as soon as we suffer a little defeat. The Lord has prepared a way for us. He is ready to use us. As soon as His hand is upon us, however, we become unhappy. Either we argue with Him, or we complain about everything to Him. From the day we were saved, the Lord has been working on us in many different ways for the purpose of breaking the self. We may or may not know it, but the Lord's goal is always to break our outer man.

The treasure is in the earthen vessel. Who needs to see your earthen vessel? The church lacks the treasure, not the earthen vessels. The world lacks the treasure, not the earthen vessels. If the earthen vessel is not broken, who will find the treasure within? The Lord works in us in so many different ways for the purpose of breaking the earthen vessel, the alabaster flask, the outer shell. The Lord wants to prepare a way to bring His blessing to the world through those who belong to Him. This is a way of blessing, but it is also a way stained with blood. Blood must be shed, and wounds are unavoidable. How crucial the breaking of this outer man is! Unless the outer man is broken, there cannot be any spiritual work. If we are consecrated to the Lord for His service, we have to be prepared to be broken by Him. We cannot excuse ourselves or preserve ourselves. We have to allow the Lord to break our outer man completely so that He can have a free way through us.

We all have to find out God's intention for us. It is unfortunate that many people do not know what the Lord is doing in them or what the Lord intends for them. May every one of us know the Lord's intention for us. When the Lord opens our eyes, we will see that everything that has happened to us throughout our lives is meaningful. The Lord never does anything in vain. After we realize that the Lord's goal is to break our outer man, we will realize that everything that has happened to us is significant. The Lord is trying to achieve one goal: To break and dismantle our outer man.

The trouble with many is that before the Lord is able to move even a finger, they show signs of displeasure already. We must realize that all the experiences, difficulties, and trials from the Lord are for our highest good. We cannot ask for anything better; they are the best. If anyone goes to the Lord and says, "Lord, please let me choose the best," I believe the Lord will tell him, "I have given you the best. What you are facing every day is for your highest good." The Lord has arranged everything for us for the purpose of breaking our outer man. We can put our spirit to full use only as our outer man is broken and our spirit is released.

BREAKING AND TIMING

The Lord breaks our outer man in two ways. First, He breaks it in a cumulative way, and second, He breaks it in a sudden way. The Lord gives some people a sudden breaking first, followed by more gradual breakings; the sudden work comes first and the cumulative work follows. Other people face situations and problems every day. Then one day, they suddenly receive one great blow from the Lord; the cumulative work comes first and the sudden work follows. These are different patterns of breaking that we ordinarily experience. Either the sudden breaking comes, followed by the cumulative breaking, or it is the other way around. Generally speaking, even with those who have not deviated and detoured, the Lord has to spend a few years before He can complete this breaking work.

We cannot reduce the time this breaking takes, but we can extend this time. The Lord completes the work in some in a few years. However, with others, the work is not completed after ten or twenty years. This is a very solemn matter! Nothing is more pitiful than wasting God's time. Too often the church is deprived of blessing because of us! We can preach with our mind and incite people with our emotion, but we cannot exercise our spirit. God cannot use His Spirit to touch others through us. When we delay the work, we incur great loss.

If we have never consecrated ourselves to the Lord in a thorough way in the past, we have to do it now. We have to say, "Lord, for the sake of the church, for the going on of the gospel, for You to have a way, and for the sake of my going on in my own life, I commit myself unreservedly and unconditionally to Your hand. Lord, I gladly put myself in Your hand. I am willing to let You find a way to release Yourself through me."

THE MEANING OF THE CROSS

We have heard about the cross for a long time. We may be very familiar with it already, but what is the cross? The meaning of the cross is the breaking of the outer man. The cross puts the outer man to death and breaks open the shell. The cross destroys everything of the outer man. It destroys our opinions, methods, wisdom, self-love, and everything. Once the outer man is broken, the inner man is released, and the spirit is able to function. The way before us is very clear indeed.

Once our outer man is broken, it becomes easy to release our spirit. One brother has a good mind; those who know him all acknowledge this. His will is strong and his emotions are reserved and deep. Yet when others meet him, they realize that they are touching his spirit, not his strong will, good mind, or reserved and deep emotions. Every time others fellowship with him, they touch a spirit, a pure spirit because this man is broken. Another sister is quick. Everyone who knows her realizes this. She is quick in thoughts, quick in words, quick to confess, quick to write, and quick to throw away what she has written. But when others meet her, they do not touch her quickness but her spirit. Her very person has been broken. The breaking of the outer man is a very fundamental issue. We cannot hold on to our weaknesses all the time. We cannot have the same flavor after the Lord has dealt with us for five or ten years. We must allow the Lord to have a way through us. This is the Lord's basic requirement of us.

TWO REASONS FOR NOT BEING BROKEN

Why do so many people remain unchanged after being dealt with for years? Others have a strong will, strong emotions, or a strong mind, yet the Lord can still break them. There are two main reasons that many people are not broken in spite of the passing of years.

First, these ones are living in darkness. They do not see God's hand. God is working and breaking, yet they do not know that God is doing the work. They are short of light, and they are not living in the light. They only see men, thinking that men are opposing them. Or they only see the environment, complaining that it is too harsh. They put all the blame on the environment. May the Lord grant us the revelation to see God's hand. May we kneel down and say, "This is You. This is You. I accept it." At a minimum we have to know whose hand is dealing with us. At a minimum we have to know *that* hand and see that it is not the world, our family, or the brothers and sisters in the church who are dealing with us. We have to see God's hand. God is the One who is dealing with us. We have to learn from Madam Guyon, who would kiss such a hand and treasure such a hand. We must have this light. We have to accept and believe everything that the Lord has done. He can never be wrong in what He does.

Second, a person is not broken because he loves himself too much. Self-love is a great obstacle to breaking. We have to ask God to remove all self-love from us. When God plucks this self-love from us, we have to worship Him, saying, "Lord! If this is Your hand, I accept it from my heart." We have to remember that all misunderstandings, complaints, and dissatisfactions arise from only one thing—secret self-love. Because we love ourselves secretly, we try to save ourselves.

This is a big problem. Many times problems arise because we try to save ourselves.

Those who know the Lord go to the cross without taking the vinegar mingled with gall! Many go to the cross reluctantly. They try to taste the vinegar mingled with gall in an attempt to relieve their feelings. Those who say, "The cup which the Father has given me, shall I not drink it?", will not take a cup that is filled with vinegar mingled with gall. They only take one cup, not both cups. These ones do not have any self-love in them. Self-love is the root of our problem. May the Lord speak within us today, and may we pray, "My God! I now see that everything comes from You. My experiences of the past five, ten, or twenty years have all come from You. All of these things were done with only one purpose in mind—that Your life would be expressed through me. I have been foolish. I did not see this. Through self-love I have done many things to save myself, and I have wasted much of Your time. Today I see Your hand, and I willingly consecrate myself to You. I commit myself to Your hand once again."

EXPECTING WOUNDS

No person expresses more charm than one who has passed through such a breaking process. A stubborn and self-loving person becomes charming after he is broken by God. Consider Jacob in the Old Testament. He wrestled with his brother from the time they were in their mother's womb. He was a naughty, cunning, and conniving person. Yet he went through many sufferings throughout his lifetime. In his youth he ran away from home and was cheated by Laban for twenty years. His beloved wife Rachel died on the way home, and his cherished son Joseph was sold. Many years later Benjamin was detained in Egypt. Jacob was dealt with by God again and again, and he met with numerous misfortunes. He was smitten by God time after time. Jacob's history is a history of God's smiting. After repeated dealings by God, he changed. During his final years, he became a truly transparent person. How dignified he was in Egypt when he stood before Pharaoh and spoke to him! At his deathbed he worshipped God leaning on his staff. How beautiful this picture is! How clear his blessing to his children and grandchildren was! In reading the last part of his history, we cannot help but bow down and worship God. Here was a matured person, one who knew God. After being dealt with for decades, Jacob's outward man was broken. In his old age we see a beautiful picture. All of us have something of Jacob in us. Perhaps more than a little! Hopefully the Lord will find a way through us. May our outer man be broken to such an extent that the inner man can be released and expressed. This is precious, and this is the way of the servants of the Lord. We can only serve when we have reached this point, and we can only lead others to the Lord and to the knowledge of God when we have reached this point. Nothing else will work. Doctrines and theology will not work. Mere Bible knowledge will not profit us. The only thing that is useful is for God to come out of us.

When our outer man is smitten, dealt with, and humbled by all kinds of misfortune, the scars and wounds that are left behind will be the very places from which the spirit flows out from within. I am afraid that some brothers and sisters are too whole; they have never suffered any dealings and have never changed in any way. May the Lord be merciful to us and set a straight course before us. May we see that this is the only way. May we see that all of the dealings that we have received from the Lord during the past ten or twenty years are for achieving this one goal. Therefore, we should not despise the Lord's work in us. May the Lord truly show us the meaning of the breaking of the outer man. Unless the outer man is broken, everything we have is in the mind and in the realm of knowledge and is useless. May the Lord grant us a thorough dealing.

Chapter Two

BEFORE AND AFTER THE BREAKING

The breaking of the outer man is a basic experience which every servant of the Lord must go through. God has to break our outer man before we can render any effective service to Him.

A servant of the Lord faces two possibilities in working for the Lord. First, his outer man is never broken and his spirit is never aroused. His spirit cannot be released, and no power flows out from it. Only his mind or his emotions are active. If he is a clever person, his mind is active. If he is a sentimental person, his emotions are active. This kind of work does not bring anyone to God. Second, it is possible that his outer man is not separated clearly from his inner man. When his spirit is released, it is wrapped in his mind or his emotions. The result is mixture and impurity. This kind of work produces mixed and impure experiences in others. These two conditions frustrate a man from serving the Lord in a proper way.

"IT IS THE SPIRIT WHO GIVES LIFE"

If we want to engage ourselves in effective works, we have to have a basic acknowledgment of one thing at least once: "It is the Spirit who gives life" (John 6:63). If we do not settle this issue this year, we will have to settle it next year. If we do not settle it the first day we believe in the Lord, we will have to settle it sooner or later, even if it is ten years later. Many people have to be brought to the end of themselves and realize the vanity of their work before they see the futility of their many thoughts and feelings. No matter how many people can be gained through our thoughts and feelings, the result is vain. Sooner or later we have to confess, "It is the

Spirit who gives life." Only the Spirit can give life. Even our best thoughts and feelings cannot give life. A man can have life only through the Spirit. The Lord's word is always true. What gives life is the Spirit. Many workers of the Lord have to go through many pains and failures before they see this fact. Since the Spirit alone gives life, it is only as the spirit is released that sinners are regenerated and believers are built up. Regeneration is a matter of transmission of life resulting in others receiving life, while building up is also a matter of the transmission of life resulting in believers being built up. Without the Spirit there can be no regeneration, and there can be no building up.

The interesting thing is that God has no intention to separate His Spirit from our spirit. In many places in the Bible it is impossible to say whether the spirit being spoken of refers to the human spirit or God's Spirit. Even many Greek experts cannot tell the difference. Throughout the ages Bible translators, from Luther in Germany to the translators of the King James Version, have been unable to ascertain which of the many references to the spirit in the New Testament denote the human spirit and which denote God's Spirit.

Romans 8 is perhaps the chapter with the most references to the word *spirit*. Who can tell which words refer to the human spirit and which refer to God's Spirit? When Bible translators come to Romans 8, they leave the readers to decide for themselves which *spirit* refers to the human spirit and which refers to God's Spirit. When the English versions come to the word *pneuma,* some use an upper-case Spirit, and others use a lower-case spirit. All versions differ in this respect, and no one person's view is authoritative. The truth is that it is impossible to differentiate between the Holy Spirit and man's spirit. When we received a new spirit, we received God's Spirit at the same time. When our human spirit was revived from its deadened state, we received the Holy Spirit at the same time. The Holy Spirit resides in our spirit, but it is difficult to tell which is the Holy Spirit and which is our spirit. There is a distinction between the Holy Spirit and our spirit, but the two are not separate. Hence, the release of the spirit is not merely a release of man's spirit but a release of the Holy Spirit through man's spirit, because the two spirits are one. We can differentiate the two spirits as terms but not in fact. The release of the spirit is the release of the human spirit. It is also the release of the Holy Spirit. When others touch our spirit, they are touching the Holy Spirit at the same time. If we can provide others the opportunity to touch our spirit, we should thank the Lord because they are being provided with an opportunity to touch God's Spirit at the same time. In fact, our spirit brings God's Spirit to men.

When God's Spirit operates, He has to operate through the human spirit. This is similar to electricity that runs household appliances; it cannot travel like the lightning in the air. It travels through the electrical wires. Today we not only have electrical power but electrical wires. The wire bears the electricity. In physics there is such a thing as an *electrical charge*. To be charged is to bear a burden. If we are to carry electricity, we have to carry the charge by means of electrical wires. This same principle holds true for God's Spirit. He needs the human spirit as a medium to bear His Spirit. Through the human spirit the Holy Spirit is conveyed and carried to men.

After a man is saved, the Holy Spirit resides in his spirit. Whether or not a man can be used by the Lord depends more on his outer man than on his spirit. The problem with some people is that their outer man has never been broken. There is not a blood-stained pathway; there is no wound, no scar. The result is that God's Spirit is locked up within their spirit and cannot be released. Sometimes the outer man moves, but the inner man does not respond. The outer man is released, but the inner man is still bound.

A FEW PRACTICAL CONSIDERATIONS

Let us consider a few practical matters. First, in the matter of preaching, we often preach earnestly, persuasively, and logically. Yet within us we are ice cold. We try to convince others, but we cannot even convince ourselves. The outer man is working, but the inner man does not join in. The outer man and the inner man do not match; they are not in unison. The outer man is excited, but the inner man remains ice cold. We tell others how great the Lord's love is, but we do not have the slightest feeling within us. We can tell others of the pain of the cross, but when we return to our room, we have no problem laughing. It is a hopeless situation when the outer man and the inner man are not in union. The outer man may be working, but the inner man is not moving at all. This is the first condition: The mind and emotions are working, but the spirit is not. The outer man acts, but the inner man does not respond. It is as if the inner man is a spectator of the outer man's performance. The outer man remains the outer man, and the inner man remains the inner man. The two are not in harmony.

At other times, the inner man can be very desperate; it wants to cry out, but it cannot utter anything. Whatever is said just beats around the bush. The more desperate the inner man becomes, the colder the outer man is. The person may want to speak, but nothing comes out. He sees a sinner and wants to cry, but no tears come out. He has an earnestness to shout on the platform, but the outer man is nowhere to be found. This is a great suffering. This frustration is the result of the outer man not being broken. As a result, the inner man is not released. When the outer shell remains, the outer man does not take orders from the inner man. When the inner man weeps, the outer man does not weep. When the inner man grieves, the outer man does not grieve. The inner man may have much to say, but the outer man does not direct its thoughts to convey them. The inner man may have many feelings, but they cannot be expressed. The spirit cannot break the outer shell.

The above descriptions fit the condition of those whose outer man is not broken. Either their spirit does not move and the outer man acts alone, or their spirit moves but the outer man blocks its passage. Therefore, the breaking of the outer man is the first lesson confronting everyone who desires to enter the service of the Lord. The fundamental training for every servant of God is to allow his inner man to come out of his outer man. Every true servant of God does not allow his outer thoughts and emotions to act independently. When his inner man needs to be released, the outer man affords a channel; the spirit can break out of the outer man to reach others. If we have not learned this lesson, our effectiveness in the work is very limited. May the Lord bring us to the place where our outer man is broken. May God show us the way to become broken before the Lord.

Once we are broken, all performances and acts will cease. We will no longer be excited outwardly and indifferent inwardly. When we have proper feelings and utterances inwardly, we will act accordingly outwardly. Nor will we experience the embarrassment of the inner man trying to weep while the outer man is unable to shed any tears. We will not complain of having things to say inwardly yet going around in circles and not being able to say them outwardly. Poverty of thoughts will not occur, and we will not need to use twenty words to utter what can be said in two words. Our mind will aid the spirit instead of frustrating it. Our emotions can be a very strong shell as well. Many people want to rejoice but cannot rejoice. They want to weep but cannot weep. The outer man will not respond. But if the Lord renders a heavy blow to the outer man through the discipline or enlightening of the Holy Spirit, they will be able to rejoice when they need to rejoice and grieve when they need to grieve. Their spirit will be released liberally and freely.

The breaking of the outer man leads to the free release of the spirit. The free release of the spirit is not only necessary to our work; it is profitable to our personal walk as well. If the spirit is released, we can constantly abide in God's presence. If the spirit is released, we spontaneously touch the spirit of inspiration that lies behind the Bible. We spontaneously receive revelation through the exercise of our spirit. If the spirit is released, we spontaneously will have power in our testimony when we deliver God's word with our spirit. We will also experience this in our preaching of God's word, that is, in ministering God's word to others as a minister of the word. Moreover, if our spirit is released, we will touch others' spirits with our spirit. When a person comes and speaks to us, we will be able to "measure him" with our spirit. We will know the kind of person he is, the kind of attitude he has, the kind of Christian life he lives, and the kind of needs he has. Our spirit will be able to touch his spirit. If our spirit is free and released, it will be easy for others to touch our spirit; our spirit will become very touchable. With some people, we can only touch their thoughts, emotions, or will; we cannot touch their spirit. They are Christians, and we are Christians, but after we sit down and talk for two or three hours, we still cannot touch them. Their outer shell is very hard, and no one can touch their inward condition. When the outer man is broken, the spirit will be open and free to flow to others, and when the spirit is open and free, others can easily touch it.

GOING AND COMING BACK

If the outer man is broken, the spirit spontaneously will remain in the Lord all the time. A brother read Brother Lawrence's book *The Practice of the Presence of God* the second year after he was saved. He struggled very much because he was not able to enjoy God's presence continually like Brother Lawrence. He made a pact with a brother to pray once every hour. He wanted to follow the biblical teaching of praying unceasingly. Every time the clock struck the hour, they would try to kneel down to pray. Nevertheless, they felt as if they could not maintain God's presence, and they wrestled to turn back to God all the time. It was as if they wandered away from God whenever they went about their own business or became engaged in their studies so that they had to hurriedly turn back to God. If they did not turn back, they felt that they would be gone forever. They prayed all the time. On Sundays they prayed the whole day, and on Saturdays they prayed half of the day. They did this for two or three years. But even though they felt His presence when they turned back to God, they would lose it as soon as they turned away. The problem of maintaining God's presence with human memory is a great frustration to many Christians, not just to these brothers. To them, the "presence" of God can only be maintained when their memory is fresh; when their memory

fails, the "presence" is gone. Such attempts to preserve the
divine presence with human memory are foolish. God's presence is in the spirit, not in the memory.

In order to deal with God's presence, we have to first deal
with the matter of the breaking of the outer man. The nature
of our emotion is different from the nature of God; the two
can never be joined as one. The same can be said of our mind.
John 4 shows us that God's nature is Spirit. Only our spirit
is of the same nature as God, and only our spirit can be in
harmony with God forever. If we try to retain God's presence
in our mind, this presence is lost as soon as we are not in
complete control of our mind. If we try to retain God's
presence in our emotion, the same is true; this presence is
gone as soon as we are not in complete control of our emotion.
Sometimes when we are happy, we think we have God's
presence. But this happiness does not stay. When it goes
away, our sense of His presence is gone. We may think that
we have God's presence when we weep, but we cannot weep
all the time. Sooner or later our tears will stop, and when
they stop, God's presence seemingly stops as well. The
function of the mind and the function of the emotion are
both activities, and no activity can go on forever. If we try
to maintain God's presence with activity, this presence will
be gone as soon as the activity stops. Two substances will
blend together only when they are of the same nature, such
as water with water or air with air. Things with the same
nature can enjoy each other's presence. The inner man is of
the same nature as God; therefore, it can realize God's presence through His Spirit. The outer man is constantly in the
realm of activity; therefore, it is a frustration to the inner
man. The outer man is not a help but a hindrance. The inner
man will be free from distractions only when the outer man is
broken.

God has installed a spirit within us to respond to Him.
The outer man, however, only responds to outward signals. A
man loses God's presence and the enjoyment of it because his
outer man is constantly responding to outside activity. We
cannot eliminate all outward signals, but the outer man can
be broken. We cannot stop all outside activity. Millions

and billions of things in this world are occurring outside of us. If the outer man is not broken, we will react whenever something happens outside of us. We cannot enjoy God's presence calmly and continually because the outer man is constantly reacting. God's presence is based on the breaking of the outer man.

If God grants us mercy and breaks our outer man, we will manifest the following traits: Our old curiosity will be dead; we will no longer be curious. Formerly, we were very strong in our emotion; we were easily stirred up in the tender sentiment of love or in the raw sentiment of anger whenever something happened. We reacted as soon as something happened around us, and we were caught up in those things. As a result, we lost God's presence. But if God is merciful to us, He will break our outer man, and our inner man will no longer be touched when many things happen to us. We will remain calm, and God's presence will abide with us.

We must see that the enjoyment of God's presence is based on the breaking of the outer man. A man can only enjoy God's uninterrupted presence when his outer man is broken. Brother Lawrence worked in a kitchen. Many people would come and demand service from him. There was noise all around him; plates were shuffled back and forth. Yet Brother Lawrence was not affected by all these things. He had God's presence when he prayed, and he also had God's presence when he was busily working. How could he maintain God's presence in the midst of his hectic work? The secret is that no outward noise could affect his inward being. Some people lose God's presence because they are inwardly affected as soon as they hear any noise around them.

Some who do not know God try to hold on to God's presence. What do they do? They look for an environment where there is "no shuffling of plates." They think that the farther away they are from people and activities, the closer they will be to God's presence. They are mistaken. They think that the problem is with the "plates," the human distractions. No, the problem is with them. God is not delivering us from the "plates"; He is delivering us from being influenced by them. Everything around us can be in turmoil, but within we can remain untouched. Everything around us can be clamorous, but within we can be perfectly still. Once the Lord breaks our outer man, our inner being will not respond to such things; we will have a deaf ear to these noises. Thank God that we can have very sensitive ears. However, the action of grace and the operation of His work will break our outer man, and nothing that comes upon our outer man will affect us any longer. When the "plates" clamor, we can hide ourselves in God's presence as much as when we are praying by ourselves alone.

Once the outer man is broken, a man does not have to come *back* to God because he is with God all the time. There is no need for a coming *back*. An unbroken man needs to come back to God whenever he goes about with his business because he has moved away. This is the reason he has to come back. A broken man never moves away; therefore, he does not need to come back. Many people move away all the time, even while they are working for the Lord. This is because their outer man has never been broken. It is best that they not do anything at all. As soon as they do something, they move away. But those who know God in a genuine way never move away. Therefore, they never need to come back. If they spend the whole day praying to God, they enjoy His presence. If they spend the whole day busily scrubbing the floor, they still enjoy His presence. As soon as our outer man is broken, we will live before God. We will not need to come back. There will not be the feeling nor need to come back.

We usually feel God's presence only when we come to Him. Whatever we do, even when we exercise the utmost care, we feel that we have turned away from God a little. I am afraid that this is most of our experience. Although we conscientiously try to rein ourselves in, we turn away as soon as we engage in some activity. Many brothers and sisters feel that they have to drop the things they have in their hands before they can pray. They somehow feel that there is a difference between being in God and doing some form of work. For example, we may be helping a person by preaching the gospel to him or by edifying him. Halfway through our conversation, we may feel that we have to pray and come back to God. We feel that we have somehow drifted from God in talking to others and that by praying we can come back to Him once more. It seems as if we have moved and are returning to God. We have lost His presence, and now we are regaining it. We may be conducting some daily chores such as scrubbing the floor or working at some craft. After we are finished with this work, we feel that we have to come back before we can pray. We feel that there is a great distance between where we are and where we want to be. Any feeling of coming back is a sign that we have moved. The breaking of the outer man will bring us to the point where we will not have to come back any longer. We will feel as much of God's presence in talking to others as when we are kneeling down and praying with them. We will feel as much of God's presence in scrubbing the floor and working on our craft as when we are praying. These things will not take us away from God's presence any longer. As a result, we will no longer need to come back.

Let me give a more extreme example. The most raw sentiment a man can have is temper. The Bible does not say that we cannot be angry; some forms of anger are unrelated to sin. The Bible says that we should "be angry, yet do not sin" (Eph. 4:26). This shows that a person can become angry without sinning. Yet anger is a very raw sentiment. In fact, it is close to sinning. God's Word never says that we should love yet not sin, because love is far from sin. Nor does God's Word say that we should be patient yet not sin, because patience is also far from sin. But God's Word says, "Be angry, yet do not sin." This shows that anger is very close to sin. Sometimes a brother commits a big mistake, and we have to rebuke him. But this is a very hard thing to do. It is easy to exercise kindness but very hard to exercise anger. Once we are careless, we will fall into a different state. It is not easy to be angry according to God's will. If we know the breaking of the outer man, we can enjoy God's continual presence without interruption from the outer man, whether we are rebuking a brother severely or praying in the presence of God. Putting this a different way, we will not have the feeling that we are turning back to God when we pray after rebuking a brother severely. Any feeling of turning back to God is a proof that we have left God. I admit that rebuking a brother is a difficult thing to do, but if our outer man is broken, we can rebuke a brother without the need of turning back to God because God's presence will be with us all the time.

THE SEPARATION OF THE OUTER MAN
FROM THE INNER MAN

When the outer man is broken, all outward activities are confined to the outward realm while the inner man continues to enjoy God's presence. The problem with many people is that their outer man and inner man are entangled together. Whatever affects the outer man affects the inner man. Strictly speaking, the outward things can only affect the outer man; but the outer man, in turn, affects the inner man. With those who are not yet broken, their outer man can affect their inner man. With those who are broken, their outer man cannot affect their inner man. If God is merciful to us and if our outer man is broken, it will be separated from our inner man, and outward things will only affect the outer man; they will not affect the inner man. When the outer man is separated from the inner man, all distractions are confined to the outer realm; they cannot enter the inner realm. A man can converse with others with his outer man while his inner man is still fellowshipping with God. The outer man can be conscious of the "shuffling of the plates," while the inner man continues to live before God. He can work and labor with his outer man, interact with the myriads of things in the outer world, yet confine all the activities to just that realm. His inner man is not affected, and he can continue to live before God. He has never left; therefore, he never needs to return. Suppose a brother is building a road. If his outer man is separated from his inner man, outward things will not affect his inner being. He can work with his outer man while his inner man is turned to God continually. Some parents can laugh and play with their children according to their outer man, but when the occasion calls for them to take up spiritual work, they can exercise their inner man immediately. Their inner man has never left God. The separation of our outer man from our inner man is very much related to our work and our life. This is the only way we can continue in our work without the need to come back to God all the time.

Some people live as one person, one entity. Others live as two persons. With some people, the outer man and the inner man are one person, one entity. With others, the two are separate. What happens to those who are one person in themselves? When they attend to their affairs, their whole being is involved in the work, and they move away from God. When they pray, they have to drop what they are doing and turn their whole being back to God. They need to apply their whole being to their work, and they need to apply their whole being to pray to God. Such ones move away all the time and need to turn back all the time. Their outer man has not yet been broken. Those who are broken by the Lord will find that their outer man no longer influences their inner man. They can take care of outward things with their outer man, while at the same time continue to abide in God and in His presence. Whenever the need arises for them to demonstrate their inner man before men, they can do so with ease; they are not cut off from the presence of God. The issue, therefore, is whether we are one person or two. In other words, is our outer man separated from our inner man? This difference is very great.

If God is merciful to us and we have such an experience of separation, we will conduct business and move around in our outer man, but our inner man will be unmoved. One person moves around, while the other person is still before God. The outer man will only mind the outward things, and the outward things will stop with the outer man; they will not get to the inner man. Those who know God apply the outer man to outward affairs while their inner man remains in God. The two men do not mix. They are like Brother Lawrence, who was busy with outward affairs, yet who had another person within him who lived before God. God's presence never went away in him. This can save us much time in our work. Many people do not have this separation of the outer man from the inner man. As a result, their whole being moves away at one time, and then they move their whole being back later. Many people face difficulties with their work because their inner man tags along with their outer man. If the inner man is separated from the outer man and remains untouched while the outer man is involved in business, many outward things will be properly handled. This kind of exercise will isolate us from the influence of the flesh through outward things; they will no longer touch our inner being.

Simply put, whether or not man's spirit can be useful to God depends on two kinds of work of the Lord. One work is the breaking of our outer man. The other work is the separating of our spirit from our soul or the dividing of our inner man from our outer man. God must accomplish these two things in us before we can put our spirit to use. The breaking of the outer man is accomplished through the discipline of the Holy Spirit, and the separation of the outer man from the inner man is through the revelation of the Holy Spirit.

CHAPTER THREE

THINGS IN THE HANDS

Let me first explain the title of this chapter. Suppose a father wants his son to do something for him. The father gives the order, but the son says, "I have something in my hands. When I am finished with what is in my hands, I will do what you want me to do." This is the meaning of having something in one's hands. Before the father asks the son to do something, the son already has something in his hands. Every one of us has something in our hands. In our course of following the Lord, we often are hindered by things in our hands. We have to tend to the things in our hands first. As a result, God's assignment is delayed. It is hard to find a person who does not have anything in his hands. We always have things in our hands prior to God's speaking, and we always have many things in our hands before the outer man is broken. The outer man is involved in business, things, labor, and activities. When God's Spirit operates in our spirit, it becomes impossible for our outer man to meet the demands. The things in our hands disqualify us from being useful spiritually in any real way.

THE OUTER MAN BEING LIMITED IN STRENGTH

Our outer man's strength is limited. Suppose a brother is not very strong and can only lift fifty catties of weight [Translator's note: a Chinese measure of weight]. If he has fifty catties on his shoulder, he cannot add ten catties. He is limited. He is not unlimited in the things he can carry. He can carry fifty catties and cannot add ten more. These fifty catties are the things in his hands. This is an analogy. The strength of our outer man is limited, just as the strength of our body is limited.

Many people realize that the strength of their body is limited. But they do not see that the strength of their outer man is also limited. As a result, they squander and waste the strength of their outer man. Suppose a person expends all his love on his parents. He will have no strength to love the brothers or to love all men. He only has so much strength, and when he has exhausted his strength, he has no more strength to spend on other things.

A man's mental strength is also limited. No one has an unlimited supply of mental energy. If a man spends more time in one thing, that is, if his mind is set fully on one thing, he will have no strength to think about other things. Romans 8 tells us that the law of the Spirit of life has freed us from the law of sin and of death. Why then is the law of the Spirit of life not working in some people? The Bible also shows us that the righteousness of the law is fulfilled in those who walk according to the spirit. In other words, the law of the Spirit of life only has an effect on those who are spiritual. The spiritual ones are those who set their mind on spiritual things. Those who set their mind on spiritual things do not have their mind set on the flesh. Only those who do not set their mind on the flesh can set their mind on spiritual things. The expression *setting the mind on* can also be translated as "paying attention to" or "taking care of." Suppose a mother leaves the house and entrusts her young child to a friend, saying, "Please take care of her for me." What does it mean to take care of the child? It means to pay attention to her all the time. A man can only pay attention to one thing; he cannot pay attention to two things at the same time. If a person commits a child to our care, we cannot take care of it on the one hand and take care of the sheep and cows on the mountain on the other hand. If we take care of the child, we cannot take care of anything else. Only those who do not take care of the things of the flesh are able to take care of the things of the spirit, and only those who take care of the things of the spirit receive the benefit of the law of the Spirit. Our mental strength is limited. If we waste our mental strength on the things of the flesh, we will not have enough mental energy to take care of the things of the spirit. If we set our mind on the things of the flesh, we will have no further strength to set our mind on the things of the spirit.

We must be very clear about this one thing: Our outer man is limited in strength, in the same way that our two arms are limited in their strength. Therefore, if there are already things in our hands, we cannot take up God's things. How much we have in our hands is inversely proportional to the power we have in our service to God. The things we have in our hands are a great hindrance, a very great frustration.

Suppose a man has "things in his hands" with respect to his emotion. He has all kinds of distracting desires and expectations. He wants and craves many things. He has so many things in his hands. When God has need of him, he has no emotions to spare because all of his emotions are used up. If he has used up all of his emotions within the last two days, he will be unable to feel or say anything for another two days. Our emotions are limited; we cannot draw from them endlessly.

Some people have a strong will; they are very determined. We may think that they have unlimited strength in their will. But even the strongest person finds himself with a wavering will when it comes to making a decision before the Lord. He will wonder if one choice is as good as another. He may appear to be a strong person, but when a situation calls for the genuine exercise of the will in the course of God's business, he cannot do it. Many people like to express their opinions. They have an opinion for everything. One minute they have one opinion; the next minute they have another opinion. They are never short of opinions. But when it comes to making a judgment on God's will, they are very hesitant. They are lost and cannot decide because their outer man is full of "things in the hands." There are too many things before their eyes and in their hands. Their entire person is consumed by these things, and all the strength of their outer man is used up and gone.

We must see that the strength of our outer man is limited. As soon as we have things in our hands, our outer man is bound.

THE SPIRIT USING AN OUTER MAN
THAT IS BROKEN

As soon as our outer man is bound, our spirit becomes bound as well. The spirit cannot bypass the outer man to operate in others. God never bypasses man's spirit when His Spirit works in man. Nor does God allow our spirit to bypass our outer man when it operates in others. This is a very important principle, and we must be clear about it. The Holy Spirit never works on man apart from man, and our spirit can never work on man apart from our outer man. Our spirit must pass through our outer man before it can operate in others. Whenever our outer man is occupied by "things in the hands" and has exhausted its strength, we cannot participate in God's work. If our spirit does not have a way to go on, the Holy Spirit does not have a way to go on either. The outer man can block the way of the inner man. The outer man can frustrate the inner man and prevent it from coming out. This is the reason that we repeatedly emphasize the breaking of the outer man.

Once the outer man has things in its hands, the inner man has no way to break out, and God's work is frustrated. Things in the hands refer to things which are present before God's work comes into view. In other words, things in the hands are things that are unrelated to God. These things are perpetuated without God's command, power, or ordination. They are not under God's hand; rather, they are independent entities.

God has to break the outer man before He can use the inner man. He has to break our love before He can use our love to love the brothers. If the outer man is not broken, we are still doing our own things, taking our own way, and loving our own preferences. God must first break our outer man before He can use our "broken" love to love the brothers and before our love can be expanded. Once the outer man is broken, the inner man is released. The inner man must love, but it must love through the outer man. If the outer man has things in its hands, the inner man will have nothing to work through.

Our will is strong. It is not only strong; it is also stubborn. When our inner man needs the will, it cannot find it, because our will has been moving too independently and has too many things in its hands. God has to give us a heavy blow; He has to smash our will and humble us so much that we are forced to say, with our face in the dust, "Lord, I dare not think. I dare not ask. I dare not decide. I need You in everything." We must be so smitten that our will can no longer act independently. Only then can the inner man take hold of the will and use it.

If the outer man is not available, the inner man will be unemployed. Can we preach God's word if we do not have a physical body? How can we preach without a mouth? It is true that one needs the spirit to preach. But preaching also requires one's mouth. What can a person do if he only has a spirit but not a mouth? At Pentecost there was the work of the Holy Spirit. But at Pentecost there was also the dispensing of the gift of speaking. Without utterance one does not have the word to release and explain God's word. If man does not speak, God has no speaking. Man's word certainly is not God's word, but God's word is conveyed through man's word. If man does not speak, there will be no word of God. There must be man's word before there can be God's word.

Suppose a brother is preparing to speak God's word. He may have the word and a burden in his spirit, and the burden may be very heavy. But if he does not have the suitable thoughts, his burden can never be released. In the end even his burden will disappear. We do not despise the burden, but even if our entire spirit is full of burden, this burden is useless and bound up if our mind is not fruitful. We cannot save men with our burden alone. The burden in our spirit must be released through our mind. After we have a burden within us, we still need a mouth. We still need a voice and the help of the body. The trouble today is that while our inner man is available to receive a burden from God, the mind in our outer man is too busy and confused. From morning to night it is giving its own suggestions and expressing its own opinions. Under such circumstances, the spirit does not have an outlet.

Today God's Spirit must be released through man. Man's love must be available before others can see God's love. Man's thoughts must be available before others can see God's thoughts. Man's decision must be found before others can touch God's will. But the trouble with man is that his outer man is too busy with his own things. He has his own views, his own thoughts. He is too busy with himself. As a result, the inner man has no way to be released. This is the reason God has to break the outer man. This does not mean that the will has to be annihilated. However, it does mean that the "things in the hands," that is, in the will, have to be stripped so that the will no longer acts independently. It does not mean that our thoughts have to be annihilated. It means that we will no longer think according to ourselves, that we will no longer come up with all kinds of ideas or be led astray by our own wandering mind. It does not mean that our emotion is annihilated. It means that our emotion will be under the control and direction of the inner man. In this way the inner man will find a mind, an emotion, and a will that are available for use.

The spirit needs a mind, an emotion, and a will to express itself. It needs a living outer man, not a dead one, to express itself. It needs a smitten, wounded, and broken outer man, not a sealed and untouched outer man. Today the biggest obstacle is with us. God's Spirit cannot break through us. His Spirit lives in our spirit, yet He cannot come out of our spirit. Our outer man is too full; it is full of things in its hands. We have to ask God for mercy so that the outer man will be broken and the inner man will have a way to come out.

God does not destroy our outer man. But neither will He allow it to remain intact and unbroken. He wants to pass through our outer man. He wants our spirit to love, think, and make decisions through the outer man. God's work can only be accomplished through a broken outer man. If we want to serve God, we have to pass through this basic dealing. If our outer man is not broken, the Lord will not be able to have a way through us. He has to break through our outer man before He can reach others.

Before the outer man is broken, the inner man and the outer man stand in opposition to one another. The inner man is a complete person, and the outer man is also a complete person. The outer man is complete and independent; it is free and full of things in the hands. Meanwhile, the inner man is imprisoned. After the outer man is genuinely broken, it no longer acts independently. It is not destroyed, but it no longer stands in opposition to the inner man; it is subject to the inner man. In this way there will be only one person left in us. The outer man will be broken into pieces and ready for the inner man's use.

Those whose outer man has been broken are "unified" men. Their outer man is under the control of the inner man. An unsaved person is also a "unified" man, but the roles of his two men are reversed: His inner man is controlled by his outer man. An unsaved person has a spirit, but his outer man is so strong that his inner man is completely subdued. At the most the inner man can voice some protest in the conscience. The inner man of an unsaved person is completely defeated and dominated by the outer man. After a man is saved, he should turn everything around. The outer man should be completely crushed and be fully under the control of the inner man. Just as an unsaved person finds his outer man dominating his inner man, we should turn things around and allow the inner man to take control of the outer man. In riding a bicycle a person can be in one of two conditions: Either the wheels work on the road or the road works on the wheels. On flat terrain, the legs peddle the wheels and the wheels work on the road. On a downward slope, the legs do not have to work. The wheels roll by themselves, and in this case, the road, that is, the slope, works on the wheels. When our inner man is strong and the outer man is broken, the wheels work on the road; that is, we decide when and how fast we want to move. But if the outer man is stubborn and unbroken, it is like riding a bicycle downhill; the slope works on the wheels. The wheels will roll by themselves, and we can do nothing about it. This is what happens when the outer man controls the inner man.

Whether or not a man is useful before the Lord depends on whether his spirit can be released through his outer man. When our inner man is bound, the outer man does everything by itself. The outer man acts independently; the wheels turn by themselves. By the Lord's grace, when He levels the slopes and breaks the outer man, the outer man no longer offers suggestions and makes decisions. When this happens, the inner man will be released freely without any hindrance from the outer man. If the Lord grants us the grace and breaks our outer man, we will become a person adept at exercising our spirit, and we will be able to release it whenever we want to.

THE PERSON, NOT THE DOCTRINES

We do not become qualified for God's work simply by learning some doctrines. The basic problem is our very person. Our person is the means by which we carry on our work. It is a matter of whether or not our person has passed through God's dealings. If the right doctrines are committed to a wrong person, what can be ministered to the church? The basic lesson for us is to make ourselves usable vessels. In order to make ourselves usable vessels, our outer man must be broken.

God has been working in us all these years. Although we are not very clear about this work ourselves, nevertheless, God has been carrying on the breaking day by day. We have gone through sufferings and difficulties for years. Time after time God's hand has halted us. We want to go one way, but God does not let us do it. We want to go another way, but God stops us again. If we do not see God's operation through the working together of all these environments, we have to pray, "God! Open my eyes so that I may see Your hand." The eyes of the donkey are often sharper than the eyes of a self-proclaimed prophet. The donkey has seen Jehovah's messenger already, but the self-proclaimed prophet has not seen it yet. The donkey realizes God's halting hand, but the self-proclaimed prophet is still ignorant of it. We have to realize that breaking is God's way with us. For years God has been trying to break our outer man. He has been trying to crush us so that we will not remain intact. Unfortunately, many people think that what they lack is doctrines. They wish they can hear more doctrines, pick up more ideas for preaching, and understand more expositions of the Bible. But this is absolutely the wrong way. God's hand is doing only one thing in us—breaking us. We cannot have our way; we have to take God's way. We cannot have our thoughts; we have to take God's thoughts. We cannot have our decisions; we have to take God's decisions. God has to break us down completely. The trouble with us is that while God stops us time after time, we blame this and that for the blockage. We are like the prophet who did not see God's hand; instead, we blame our "donkey" for halting.

Everything that comes our way is meaningful and under God's sovereign arrangement. Nothing accidental happens to a Christian. Nothing is outside God's ordering. We have to humble ourselves under God's sovereign arrangements. May the Lord open our eyes to see that God is arranging everything around us; He has a purpose in us. Through everything He is crushing us. When God grants us the grace one day, we will gladly accept all the arrangements He places in our environment. Our spirit will be released, and we will be able to use our spirit.

A LAW, NOT A MATTER OF PRAYER

In dealing with us and in breaking us for the release and exercise of the spirit, God works according to His law, not according to our prayer. What does this mean? This means that the release of the inner man through a broken outer man is a law. It is not something that we secure by means of prayer.

A law cannot be altered by prayer. If we put our hand into the fire while we pray, our hand will still be burned. (I am not speaking about miracles here. I am speaking about a natural law.) Our prayer cannot change the law. We have to learn to obey God's law. Do not think that prayer alone will work. If we do not want our hand to be burned, we should not put it in the fire. We should not pray and put our hand in the fire at the same time. God deals with us according to law. The inner man can only be released through the outer man. This is a law. If the outer man is not broken and pulverized, the inner man will not be released. This is the Lord's way. He has to break us before He can have an outlet through us. We should never challenge this law while praying for this or that blessing. Such prayers do not work. Our prayer cannot change God's law.

The way to true spiritual work is for God to be released through us. This is the only way God will take. If a man is not broken, the gospel will not go out through him, and God cannot use him. He will have no way to go on. We have to truly prostrate ourselves. Submission to God's law is better than many prayers. A minute of revelation of God's way is better than an incessant, ignorant pleading for God's blessings and His help in our works. It is better to stop such prayer and say to the Lord, "I humble myself before You." Our prayer for blessing often is nothing but a hindrance to God. We often long for blessing but do not even find mercy. We have to ask for light. We have to learn to humble ourselves under His hand and obey this law. With obedience there is blessing.

CHAPTER FOUR

HOW TO KNOW MEN

It is crucial for a worker of the Lord to be able to know men. When a person comes to us, we have to know his spiritual condition. We have to know what kind of person he was and what he has now become. We have to know what he is saying with his mouth and what he is really saying in his heart, and what is the difference between the two. We have to know what he is trying to hide from us. We have to know his outstanding characteristics, whether he is stubborn or humble, and whether his humility is real or artificial. The effectiveness of our work very much depends on our ability to discern the spiritual condition of others. If the Spirit of God shows our spirit the condition of those who come to us, we will be able to give them a suitable word.

Whenever men came to the Lord in the Gospels, He spoke a suitable word to them. This is amazing! The Lord did not speak to the Samaritan woman about the truth of regeneration. Neither did He speak to Nicodemus about the living water. The word on regeneration was for Nicodemus, and the word on the living water was for the Samaritan woman. How fitting! To those who had never followed Him, He issued a calling. To those who wanted to follow Him, He spoke of bearing the cross. To those who volunteered, He spoke of counting the cost. To those who were hesitant to follow, He spoke of letting the dead bury the dead. The Lord has a suitable word for everyone, because He knows everyone. Whether a person comes to the Lord with a seeking heart or a prying attitude, our Lord knows him. This is the reason His word is forever effective and suitable. Our Lord is far ahead of us in dealing with men. We are following Him only from a distance. Although we are following at a distance, we still have to follow;

the direction has to be the same. May the Lord be merciful to us so that we may learn to know men as He does.

If we place a soul in the hand of a brother who has no discernment of men, he will not know how to deal with him. He will only speak according to his subjectivity. If he has a certain feeling on a certain day, he will speak of this feeling to whomever he meets. If he has a favorite subject, he will speak to everyone about that subject. How can such a person do an effective work? No doctor can prescribe only one kind of medicine to all of his patients. Unfortunately, some servants of God have only one prescription. They do not understand others' illnesses, yet they try to heal them. They do not know the problem, they do not know the complexity of men, and they have never learned to know the spiritual condition of others. Nevertheless, they act as if they have a ready treatment for everyone. This is indeed foolish. We cannot expect to heal every spiritual sickness with just one spiritual prescription. This is absolutely impossible.

We should not think that those who are slow in feeling will have a difficult time discerning men, but that those who are sharp in mind will have an easy time discerning men. Neither slowness in feeling nor sharpness of mind have anything to do with discerning men. We cannot discern men with our mind or our feelings. No matter how sharp our mind is, we cannot bring the hidden things in man to light, nor can we touch the depth of man's condition.

When a worker contacts a man, the first and most basic thing for him to do is to learn what this person's real need is before God. Sometimes even the person's own answer is unreliable. When he says that he has a headache, does he really mean that only his head hurts? Perhaps the headache is merely a symptom; his sickness may not be in the head. Or he may say that he feels feverish, but this does not necessarily mean that he has a temperature. He can say many things, but the things he says may not be that reliable. Very few patients really know what is wrong with them. They do not know the kind of sickness they have. They need us to diagnose them and tell them of their need. If we want them to tell us what is wrong with them, they may not be able to tell us the right thing. Only those who have studied medicine, that is, those who are trained in discerning spiritual problems, can tell them what they need.

When we are making a diagnosis, we must know what we are speaking of. We cannot impose a diagnosis upon others. A subjective person will insist that others are sick with what he imagines the illness is; he will impose an illness upon others. When a person is sick or in difficulty, he cannot identify his problem. We have to point it out to him. Yet we should not insist on our diagnosis in a subjective way.

Whether or not we can render help to the brothers and sisters depends on whether we can identify their problems and give them the right prescription. If our diagnosis is correct, we will help them. Sometimes we may find out that their problem is beyond our ability, but at least a course of action is clear. Some spiritual conditions are within our ability to help, while others are beyond our ability to help. We should not be so foolish as to assume that we can do everything and can help everyone. Some people are within our ability to help, and we should give our whole being to help them. Some people are beyond our ability to help, and we should tell the Lord: "This is beyond my power. I cannot deal with this sickness. I have never been trained in this matter, and I cannot deal with this problem. Lord, be merciful to him!" Perhaps the specific function of some members of the Body will come to our mind, and we may realize that this is something that that brother or sister can do. We then can refer the matter to him or her. We know our own limitations, and we know that this is all we can do. We should not think that we can take every kind of spiritual work upon ourselves; we cannot monopolize everything. We have to see our limitations. At the same time, we have to know the supply in the other members. We should be able to look to them and say, "This is something beyond my ability. This is your business." This is the principle of co-working together, the principle of the Body. We can never move independently.

Every worker of the Lord and servant of God has to learn to know men. Those who do not know others' spiritual conditions are not qualified to work. It is unfortunate that the spiritual well-being of many people is ruined in the hands of inexperienced brothers. These brothers cannot render others any help. They can only impose their subjective views on them; they cannot meet the objective needs. This is our most serious problem. Others are not sick in a certain way just because we think that is their sickness. Whatever their spiritual condition may be, they are what they are. Our responsibility is to learn their spiritual condition. If we are not properly calibrated, we will not be able to render help to other children of God.

THE TOOL TO KNOW PEOPLE

When a doctor diagnoses a patient, he needs the help of many instruments. We, however, do not have any instruments. We do not have any thermometers or X-ray machines. We do not have any physical instruments to measure the spiritual condition of others. How can we decide whether or not a brother is sick? How can we diagnose him? This is where God's work comes in. God must turn our whole being into the very standard of measurement. God has to work on us to the extent that we can measure others to determine whether they are sick and to determine the nature of their sickness. This is how the Lord uses us. This work is much more difficult than the work of a doctor. We have to have a deep realization of the grave responsibility that faces us.

Suppose a doctor does not have a thermometer. The doctor then would have to feel the patient with his hand to determine whether or not he has a fever. His hand would have to function as a thermometer. If this were the case, his hand would need to be very sensitive indeed. It would not only need to be sensitive but accurate as well. This is exactly what is going on in spiritual work. We are the thermometers; we are the medical instruments. Therefore, we have to go through strict trainings and dealings. What is untouched in us will remain untouched in others. We can never expect to help others in the areas that we ourselves have not first learned the lessons. The first matter we have to settle is whether or not we have learned the lesson before the Lord. The more completely and thoroughly we learn our lessons, the more useful we will be to God's work. The less we learn, that is, the less price we pay and the more we hold back ourselves, our pride, our narrowness, our opinions, and our joy, the less useful we will be. If we spare and save these things in ourselves, we will be unable to deal with them in others. A proud person cannot deal with a proud person. A narrow person cannot deal with a narrow person. A spurious person cannot deal with a spurious person. A loose person cannot deal with a loose person. If we are a certain kind of person and are afraid of condemning that kind of illness in others, we will be unable to know whether or not others have a similar illness, much less help them. It is possible that a medical doctor can heal others but cannot heal himself. In spiritual matters, however, the same principle does not apply. First the worker is the patient; he must be healed of the sickness before he can heal others who have the same sickness. He cannot make others see what he has never seen himself. He cannot make others experience what he has never experienced himself. He cannot make others learn the lessons that he has never learned himself.

Before the Lord we have to see that we are the very instruments which God uses to discern men. Therefore, our very person must be very reliable. Our feelings and judgment must be very reliable. In order for our feelings to be reliable, we have to pray, "Lord! Do not let me go." In order for our feelings to be reliable, we have to allow God to perform works that we have never dreamed of. We have to allow God to work on us to such an extent that we become useful to Him. If a thermometer cannot accurately gauge temperature, a doctor cannot use it. A thermometer has to be reliable and accurate. When we try to identify others' spiritual problems, we are facing an issue far more serious than identifying physical illnesses. Yet we have our own thoughts, feelings, opinions, and ways. One minute we try to do one thing and the next minute we try to do something else. Because we are unreliable and unusable, we have to go through God's dealing before we can become useful.

Do we feel the gravity of our responsibility? God's Spirit does not work directly on man. He only works through some men. Although the discipline of the Holy Spirit does bring a person what he needs, nevertheless, God works through the minister's speaking, that is, through the ministry of the word. Without the ministry of the word, the spiritual problems of the brothers and sisters will remain. This responsibility is upon us. This is a very sober matter. Whether or not we, the person, can be used by God directly affects the supply that comes to the church.

Suppose a certain illness always results in a temperature of 103 degrees Fahrenheit. We cannot feel the patient with our hand and say, "This roughly feels like 103 degrees." We have to be very accurate and certain that it is 103 degrees before we can say that he has an illness that is associated with this temperature. God is using us, the person, to diagnose others' sicknesses. It is too risky for us to diagnose others if our feelings, thoughts, opinions, or spiritual understandings are wrong, or if we have not learned enough from the Lord. But if we are accurate and reliable persons, ones whom God can trust, His Spirit will flow out of us.

The beginning of all spiritual work is based on our repeated calibration before the Lord. A thermometer must be made according to certain specifications. It must be carefully checked according to the standard before it will give reliable and accurate readings. We are like the thermometer. If we are not accurate, we will only bring in confusion. In order for us to be accurate, we have to be calibrated through fine dealings. We are the doctors, and we are the instruments as well. Therefore, we have to learn our lessons properly.

THE WAY TO KNOW MEN— FROM THE SIDE OF THE PATIENT

In order to know the condition of a patient, we have to consider this matter from two sides: From the side of the patient and from our side.

From the side of the patient, how can we determine his sickness? If we want to know a person's sickness, we have to find the most conspicuous and unusual point about him. The unusual point is the most obvious point. No matter how hard he tries to hide it, he cannot keep it out of sight. A proud person will be found in his pride. Even when he is acting humbly, his humility still exposes his pride. He cannot hide it. A sad person conveys his sadness even when he smiles. The kind of person a man is dictates the kind of expression he displays and the kind of impression he gives to others. This is a fact.

The Bible describes man's spiritual condition in many ways. Some have a spirit of wrath; others have a spirit of stubbornness or a contrite spirit. In fact, we can use all kinds of words to describe man's spiritual condition. We can say that a man has a frivolous spirit or a downtrodden spirit, etc. What is the source of all of these spiritual conditions? For example, when we say that the spirit is stubborn, where does this stubbornness come from? When we say that the spirit is proud, where does this pride come from? When we say that the spirit is wild, where does this wildness come from? A normal spirit has no characteristic of its own. It has no characteristic other than to manifest God's Spirit. We speak of a stubborn spirit, a proud spirit, a haughty spirit, an unforgiving spirit, a jealous spirit, etc., because the outer man has not been separated from the inner man. The condition of the outer man is the condition of the inner man. When we say that a spirit is stubborn, we mean that the inner man of that person has assumed the characteristics of the stubborn outer man. When we say that a spirit is proud, we mean that the inner man of that person has been covered with the proud outer man. When we say that a spirit is jealous, we mean that the inner man of that person has been shrouded with the jealousy of the outer man. This occurs when the outer man and the inner man are not separated. The spirit itself has no characteristic of its own. The characteristics of the outer man have become the characteristics of the spirit. When the outer man is not broken, the spirit takes on the characteristics of the outer man.

The spirit is of God and does not have any characteristic of its own. But when our outer man is aberrant in nature, the spirit is affected. The spirit can be proud or stubborn because the condition of the outer man is mixed up with the spirit when the outer man is not broken. When the spirit is released, the condition of the outer man tags on to the spirit and is released together with the spirit. A proud person tags his pride on to his spirit and releases it together with his spirit. A stubborn person tags his stubbornness on to his spirit and releases it together with his spirit. A jealous person tags his jealousy on to his spirit and releases it together with his spirit. This is why, according to our experience, we have proud spirits, stubborn spirits, and jealous spirits. These are, strictly speaking, not characteristics of the spirit itself but characteristics of the outer man. Therefore, in order to have a clean spirit, a man does not have to deal with his spirit; he only needs to deal with his outer man. The trouble is not with the spirit but with the outer man. The characteristics a man displays when his spirit is released tell us the areas in which he is unbroken. The kind of spirit we touch in a person identifies the characteristics of his outer man. It also tells us the areas in which he has remained unbroken. He has passed these things on to his spirit, tagging them and pegging them to his spirit. As a result, his spirit is bound and shrouded with the many conditions of his outer man.

If we know how to touch others' spirit, we will know a brother's need because the secret to knowing man is to touch his spirit. We have to touch the very thing that is attached to a person's spirit. I do not mean that the spirit itself has anything that we have to touch. I mean that the spirit always carries something with it. Knowing the condition of a man's spirit means knowing the condition of his outer man. We have to repeat: This is the basic principle in knowing a person. The condition of a man's spirit is the condition of his outer man. Whatever the spirit manifests is a reflection of the state of the outer man. The characteristics of the spirit are the characteristics of the outer man. A brother may be very strong and conspicuous in a certain point, which strikes our attention as soon as we come into contact with him. It is the first thing we touch and sense, and we immediately know that it is from his unbroken outer man. Once we touch his spirit, we know his condition, and we know the things he is trying to show as well as the things he is trying to hide. We know a person by knowing his spirit.

THE WAY TO KNOW MEN—
FROM THE SIDE OF OURSELVES

What must we do before we can know the condition of man's spirit? We have to pay special attention to this point. All of the discipline we receive from the Holy Spirit is a lesson from God. Whenever the Holy Spirit disciplines us, we become more broken. As we receive more discipline, we experience more breaking. In whatever matter we receive the Spirit's discipline, we are broken in that same matter. This discipline and breaking is not once for all. Many areas in our lives require repeated discipline and breaking before we can become useful to the Lord. When we find that we can touch a brother with our spirit, it does not mean that we can touch every brother with our spirit, nor does it mean that we can touch every spiritual aspect of a brother with our spirit. It only means that as we have been disciplined by the Holy Spirit and broken in a certain aspect, we are able to touch a brother in that same aspect. If we have not been broken by the Lord in a certain matter and our spirit is insensitive or unprofitable in that matter, we cannot minister to the brother's need. In other words, the discipline we receive from the Holy Spirit is proportional to our spiritual sense. The more breaking we receive, the more our spirit will be released. In whatever matter we experience the breaking, our spirit will be released in that matter. This is a spiritual fact; it can never be artificially engineered. If we have it, we have it. If we do not have it, we do not have it. This is the reason we must accept the discipline and breaking of the Holy Spirit. Those who have much experience will be able to render much service. Only those who have gone through much breaking will acquire much feeling. Only those who suffer much loss will have much to give others. If we try to save ourselves in a certain matter, we will lose our spiritual usefulness in that matter. If we try to protect or excuse ourselves in a certain matter, we will lose our spiritual sense and supply in that matter. This is a very basic principle.

Only those who have learned their lessons can participate in the service. A man can learn the lessons of ten years in one year, or he can drag out the lessons of one year for twenty or thirty years. If a man delays his learning, he delays his service. If God has given us a heart to serve Him, we must be clear about our way. The way of our service is the way of breaking; it is a way acquired through the discipline of the Holy Spirit. It is impossible for those who have never experienced the discipline of the Holy Spirit and who have never been broken to participate in the service. The amount of discipline by the Spirit and the amount of our breaking determine the amount of service. No one can change this. If a person has this experience, he has it. If he does not have it, he does not have it. Human affection and wisdom have no place here. The degree of God's work on us determines the capacity of our service. The more we are dealt with, the more we will know people. The more we experience the discipline of the Holy Spirit, the more we will be able to touch others with our spirit.

It hurts me very much to see many brothers and sisters so lacking in discernment in many spiritual things. Some are of the Lord, yet they do not know it. Others are of the natural man, yet they are ignorant of this as well. They do not know when a person is exercising his mental strength or working by his own emotion. They do not have the discernment because they are too poor in their learning. God has given us His Spirit once for all, but learning lessons in our spirit is a lifetime endeavor. The more we learn, the more we see. Once the Lord gives us a severe blow in a certain matter, we immediately will be alerted when the same seed sprouts in other brothers. It does not have to develop into a big plant; a little sprout is all that is needed for us to detect it. The extent of the Lord's work on us is the extent to which we acquire such discernment. Spiritual senses are acquired one by one, time after time. A man can only have feelings as often as he has been dealt with. Suppose a person condemns pride in his mind. He may even be able to preach on the subject of pride. But in his spirit he does not feel the evil of pride. When others are proud, he does not feel sickened. On the contrary, he seems to be full of sympathy for them. When God's Spirit operates on him, he will see what pride is. He will experience God's dealing, and the very matter of pride itself will be burned away from him. When he opens his mouth to condemn pride again, the teaching may be the same, but a basic difference will be evident. As soon as a proud spirit comes out of a brother, he will feel that something is wrong. In fact, he will feel sickened. What he has learned and seen from God will give him a sick feeling. No other word describes this feeling better than the word *sick*. From that point onward he will be able to serve this brother because he knows his illness; he has passed through the same illness and has received healing from it. Although he cannot say that he is completely healed, he can say that he has been healed a little. This is how we acquire our spiritual knowledge.

God's gift of the Holy Spirit is once for all. But acquiring spiritual senses is a continual process. The more we learn, the more feelings we acquire. The less we learn, the less feelings we have. What use is there in trying to save ourselves or preserve ourselves? Those who will save their own life will lose it. If we try to save ourselves from pain in a certain matter, we will lose the chance of gaining what the Lord wants us to gain in that same matter. We have to ask the Lord not to release us from His hand. May He work on us time after time. The saddest thing is to see the Lord working on us once, twice, with no result at all. Time after time, we are ignorant of the work of the Lord's hand. We do not pay attention to what He is doing. We even oppose His work. A man is short of spiritual understanding and discernment because he is short in spiritual learning. May we realize before the Lord that the more dealings we receive, the more knowledge we will acquire concerning men and many things, and the more we will have to offer others. In order to expand the sphere of our service, we must expand the sphere of our dealings. It is impossible to have an expanded sphere of service without an expanded sphere of dealing.

SOME PRACTICAL POINTS

After we are dealt with by the Lord and have learned our basic lessons, our spirit will be released, and we will be able to use our spirit to touch other brothers, and we will know their condition. Here we should discuss some practical steps in learning to know men.

In order to touch others' spirit, we have to let them speak. Of course, some people can touch others' spirit without waiting for them to open their mouths. But such persons are rare. Generally speaking, we have to wait for others to open their mouth. God's Word says that out of the abundance of the heart the mouth speaks. No matter what intention or tactic a man may have, what he says comes out of the abundance of his heart. If he is spurious, a spurious spirit will come out. If he is jealous, a jealous spirit will come out. We can touch a person's spirit by listening to what he says. When a man is speaking, we have to pay attention not only to the things he is saying but to the condition of his spirit. We do not know men merely by their words but by their spirits.

When the Lord Jesus was on His way to Jerusalem and two disciples saw the Samaritans rejecting Him, they said, "Lord, do You want us to command fire to come down from heaven and consume them?" Once they opened their mouths, their spirits came out. The Lord said, "You do not know of what kind of spirit you are" (Luke 9:54-55). Here the Lord showed that one's spirit can be discerned by listening to his words. As soon as words come out, the spirit is exposed. Out of the abundance of the heart the mouth speaks. Whatever the condition of the heart is, the mouth will reflect it.

In listening to others, we should pay attention not only to their story but also to their spirit. Suppose two brothers are arguing, and both say that the other is wrong. When the matter is presented to us, how should we deal with it? When the argument broke out, only the two brothers were present. We do not know what happened. But as soon as they open their mouths, we can find out something; we can know their spirits. Among Christians, wrong is not judged by mistakes in facts but by deviations in spirits. When a brother opens his mouth, we may not be able to tell if he is wrong according to facts, but we immediately can tell whether he is wrong in spirit. He may accuse others of slandering him, but his own spirit is wrong. The whole issue depends on the spirit. A person with a wrong spirit is wrong not only in the things he has done but also in his very own person. Right and wrong before God are determined by the spirit, not merely by facts. Therefore, in listening to others, we have to touch their spirit. In the church many problems are related to the spirit, not to facts. If we judge everything according to the facts, we will bring the church into another realm. We are in the realm of the spirit, not in the realm of facts. We should never be dragged away by the facts.

If our spirit is open, we will be sensitive to all kinds of spiritual conditions. Sometimes we will sense when the other party has a closed and bound spirit. At such times we have to make discernments with our spirit and learn to know him. May we be able to echo Paul's word: "We, from now on, know no one according to the flesh" (2 Cor. 5:16). We should not know men by the flesh. We should know men by the spirit. Once we learn this basic lesson, we have a way to go on in God's work.

CHAPTER FIVE

THE CHURCH AND THE WORK OF GOD

If we truly know the meaning of God's work, we will have to acknowledge that the outer man is indeed a great hindrance. We can say that God is restricted by man today. God's children must understand the function of the church and its relationship with God's power and His work.

GOD'S MANIFESTATION OR GOD'S LIMITATION

There was a time when God confined Himself within the body of a man—Jesus of Nazareth. With that flesh there was the possibility of either limiting God or manifesting God's riches. Before incarnation God's riches were not limited. But after incarnation God's work and power were limited to this flesh. God would not do anything apart from that flesh. God was willing to be limited by that flesh. Of course, the Bible shows us that God was not limited in any way by that flesh. It could have limited God, but it did not; rather, it manifested God's riches in a full way. God's riches became the riches of that flesh.

God put Himself into flesh at the time of incarnation. Today God has put Himself into the church. His power and work are found in the church. At the time of the four Gospels, God did not do anything apart from that flesh. All of His works were committed to the Son. In the same way God has entrusted all of His works to the church. He does not do anything apart from the church. God does not work independently; He works exclusively through the church. From Pentecost until today, God's work has always been carried out through the church. Just as He committed Himself wholly, unequivocally, and unreservedly to one person—Christ, He has given Himself wholly, unequivocally, and unreservedly to the church. How great the church's responsibility before God is! The church can limit God's work; it can limit God's release.

Jesus of Nazareth was God. God was manifested in Him. He did not limit God because everything within and without Him was taken up by God. His emotions were God's emotions. His thoughts were God's thoughts. While He was on earth He did not come to do His own will but the will of the One who sent Him (John 6:38). The Son did nothing from Himself; He only did what He saw the Father doing (5:19). He did not say anything from Himself. What He heard from the Father, these things He spoke to the world (8:26). In Him we see a man in whom God entrusted Himself. God could say that this was the Word becoming flesh, God becoming man in a full way. When God wanted to dispense His life to men, this One could readily respond, "If [the grain of wheat] dies, it bears much fruit" (12:24). He was able to release His life. He did not become a hindrance or a frustration. Today God has chosen the church to be His vessel. He has put Himself, His power, and His work into the church. His desire is to release Himself through the church. The church is the oracle of God, the vessel through which God manifests His power and accomplishes His work. If the church affords God a way today, God's power and work will be expressed. If the church fails, God will be limited.

The fundamental teaching of the Gospels is that God was in a man, while the fundamental teaching of the Epistles is that God is in the church. The Gospels tell us that God was only in one man. He was only in Jesus Christ. The Epistles show us that God is only in the church. He is not in any organization or congregation. He is only found in the church. May our eyes be opened to see this glorious fact.

Once our eyes are opened to this glorious fact, we will spontaneously lift our gaze heavenward and say, "My God, how I have restricted You!" When the Almighty God dwelt in Christ, He was still the Almighty One; He was not limited or diminished in any way. God's hope and goal today is that in the church He would continue to be the Almighty One, the infinite One. God wants to freely express Himself in the church just as He was expressed in Christ. If the church is restricted, God is restricted. If the church is powerless, God is powerless. This is a very serious matter. We can only speak such a word humbly and respectfully. Simply put, any obstacle in us becomes an obstacle to God. Any limitation in us becomes a limitation to God. If God is not released through the church, He does not have a way to go on. God's way today is through the church.

Why is the discipline of the Holy Spirit so important? Why is the dividing of the soul from the spirit so important? Why must the outer man be broken by the disciplining work of the Holy Spirit? It is because God needs to have a way through us. We should never think that this is merely about personal, spiritual edification. It is not merely a matter of personal, spiritual experiences. It is very much related to God's way and work. This is a big issue. Should we limit God? Does God have the liberty in us? Only as we are dealt with and broken will God find full freedom in us.

If the church is to afford God a free way, we must undergo His stripping and allow Him to break our outer man. The greatest hindrance to this is our outer man. If the matter of the outer man is not settled, the issue of the church as God's channel can never be settled. If our outer man is broken by God's grace, there is no limit to how God will employ us as channels to His work.

BREAKING AND THE WAY GOD'S WORK OPERATES

After the outer man is broken, how does a man approach God's Word, how does he serve as a minister of His word, and how does he preach the gospel? Let us turn our attention to these questions.

Studying the Word

One undeniable fact in studying God's Word is that the kind of person we are determines the kind of Bible we have in our hands. A man often approaches the Bible with his rebellious, confused, and seemingly clever mind. What he gets out of the Bible is the product of his mind; he does not touch the spirit of the Word. If we want to meet the Lord through the Bible, our rebellious and uncooperative mind must be broken. If our mind is always rebellious and uncooperative, none of our cleverness will do us any good. We may think that our cleverness is outstanding, but it is a great hindrance to God. No matter how clever we are, we can never know God's thought through our cleverness.

There are at least two things that we should do when we come to the Bible. First, our thoughts must be identified with the thoughts of the Bible. Second, our spirit must be identified with the spirit of the Bible. We have to think like the writers of the Bible. Men like Paul and John had certain thoughts behind them when they wrote the various portions of the Word. We have to get into the same thoughts. We have to begin from where they began, and develop our thoughts along the same line they developed. We have to reason the same way they reasoned, and consider the same teachings they considered. In other words, our thoughts are like a cog, and their thoughts are also like a cog. The two cogs have to interlock with one another. Our thoughts have to enter Paul's and John's thoughts. As our thoughts enter the Bible's thoughts and our mentality becomes one with the mentality behind God's inspiration, we will understand what the Bible says.

Some people read the Bible with their mind as the principal organ. They read in the hope of picking up some ideas from the thoughts in the Bible. They have a whole set of doctrines spinning in their minds already, and they only want to collect material from the Bible to strengthen their doctrines. When we stand up to speak, an experienced person, after five to ten minutes of our speaking, knows whether we are quoting Scriptures with our mind or whether our thoughts are merged with the thoughts of the Bible. These are two entirely different things. These two kinds of preaching belong to two entirely different worlds. When some stand up to preach, they may be scriptural and their sermons may be very attractive, but their thoughts are contrary to the thoughts of the Bible; the two are incompatible with each other. However, others are different. When they speak on the Bible, their thoughts are merged with the thoughts of the Bible. The two become one and are in harmony with each other. This is the right way. But not everyone can do this. In order for our thoughts to merge with the Bible's thoughts, our outer man has to be broken. If the outer man is not broken, we cannot even read the Bible. We should not think that our study of the Bible is poor because we cannot find anyone to teach us. It is poor because our very person is wrong; our thoughts have not subjected themselves to God. As soon as we are broken, we will cease our own activity. We will not have any subjective notion of our own. Gradually, faintly, and little by little, we will touch the Lord's thinking. We will touch the thoughts behind the writers of the Bible, and we will think as they did. The outer man must be broken before we can enter into the thoughts behind God's Word. When this happens, the outer man is no longer a hindrance.

It is important in our study of the Word to have our thoughts enter into the thoughts of the writers of the Bible and to have our thoughts enter into the thoughts of the Holy Spirit. However, this is only the initial step. Without this step, we cannot study the Bible at all. But even when we have made this step, we may not be reading the Bible correctly. The Bible is not made up just of thought. The most important thing about the Bible is that God's Spirit is released through this book. Peter, John, Matthew, Mark, and every writer of the Bible had the same experience: As they were writing the Bible under the inspiration of the Holy Spirit, they wrote according to a certain train of thought, but at the same time, their spirits were released along with the release of the Holy Spirit. The world can never understand that behind the words of the Scriptures there is the Spirit. When the Spirit is released, the prophets come alive, as it were, and speak to us once again. If we hear a prophet speaking today, we have to realize that his speaking contains not only words and thoughts but something else. This something is mysterious, even though within us we are clear that this "something" is the Spirit. The Bible contains not only thoughts but the release of the Spirit. Therefore, the basic and most crucial requirement of all in reading the Bible is to be able to release one's spirit to touch the spirit of the Bible. We have to strike the spirit of the Bible with our own spirit before we can understand the Bible.

Suppose a naughty boy breaks a window of a neighbor's house and the owner of the house runs out to scold the child. When the mother finds out, she will scold the child as well. But there is a different feeling associated with the scolding of the owner than with the scolding of the mother. Outwardly, both are scoldings. But the "spirits" behind the scoldings are different. The owner of the house scolds out of anger; his is a spirit of wrath. The mother's scolding is filled with love, hope, and education. Her rebuke is a rebuke of love, a rebuke of hope, and a rebuke for education. The two spirits are entirely different.

This is a simple illustration. The Spirit behind the writing of the Bible is much stronger than the kind of "spirit" mentioned above. The Spirit behind the writing of the Bible is an eternal Spirit. It is still with us today; it forever saturates the Bible. If our outer man is broken and our spirit is released, our thoughts will not only become one with the thoughts of the Bible, but our whole being will touch the very Spirit that is behind the writing of the Bible. If our spirit is not released and we are cut off from the spirit of the authors of the Bible, we will never understand God's Word; the Bible will be a dead book to us. Hence, we are back to the same fundamental issue: The outer man has to be broken. Our thoughts will become fruitful and our spirit will be free to flow only when the outer man is broken. Only then will God not be restricted by us. The problem we face today is that we are constantly frustrating God. Even in the study of the Bible we frustrate God and limit His freedom.

Ministering the Word

On the one hand, God wants us to understand His Word—this is the beginning of His work. On the other hand, He desires to place one or two words in our spirit. These words become a burden to us, and He desires that we minister these one or two words to the church. Acts 6:4 says, "But we will continue steadfastly in prayer and in the ministry of the word." Ministry is service, and the ministry of the word is a service that serves men with God's word.

What is our problem? Our problem is that we have the word within us but cannot release it. Some people have a word and a very heavy burden within their spirit. They want to convey this word to the brothers and sisters. Yet as they speak on the platform, the burden is bound within them. After speaking one or two sentences, a minute, or even an hour, the burden is still not released. The word cannot be released, and the outer man cannot convey the inward burden. They want to discharge the burden and the message that is within them, but their outer man cannot provide them with any utterance. No matter how much they speak, they feel that the burden remains unchanged. They come with a burden and leave with the same burden. The only explanation for this is that their outer man is not broken. Their outer man cannot render any help to their inner man. On the contrary, it becomes a stumbling block to the inner man.

If our outer man is broken, it is easy to say what we want to say. When we have a burden or a word within, our outer man will come up with a suitable word to fitly express our inner thoughts. As soon as the word within us is released, the burden within us is lifted as well. The more we speak, the lighter we will feel. We will realize that our work is to serve the church with God's word. Therefore, the burden within must be matched by suitable words from our thoughts without. If the outer man is not broken, it will not yield to the will of the inner man. It will not obey the inner feeling or the spirit within. When the outer man tries to probe the feeling of the inner man, it will find nothing. It will not find the necessary and suitable words, and God will not be released. God will be stalled and blocked, and the church will not receive any help.

We must remember that the outer man constitutes the greatest hindrance to the ministry of the word. Many people think that cleverness is somewhat useful. This is wrong. No matter how clever a person is, the outer man can never replace the inner man. The inner man will come up with the right thoughts and proper words to flow out only as the outer man is broken and smashed. The outer shell must be broken by God. The more this shell is broken, the more the life in the spirit will be released. If the shell remains, the burden in the spirit will remain, and God's life and power will not flow to the church. Such a person will not be able to serve as a minister of the word. God's power and life primarily are released through the ministry of the word. If the outer man is not smitten and does not have any open wounds, the inner man will have no outlet. Those who come for the message will hear sound only; they will not touch life. The speaker may be eager to deliver something, but the audience will not receive anything. He will have the word within him, but he will not be able to speak it out because his outer man is blocking the way.

We find a precious story in the life of the Lord Jesus. A person touched only the hem of His garment, and she received His strength. The hem of His garment is the outermost part of His being. This person could feel His power even in His outermost part. The problem with us is that we have God's life within us, but this life cannot flow out. We have the word within us, but we cannot release this word. We have God's word within us, but we have obstacles around us. As a result, this word cannot be released. When God does not have any freedom in us, He cannot flow freely out of us.

Preaching the Gospel

Many people have the wrong concept that a man believes in the gospel because he has heard the right teachings, or because he is touched in his emotion. But this is far from the truth. Those who base their acceptance of the Lord on emotional impulses will not last, nor will those who are convinced by persuasion in the mind. There is nothing wrong with using the mind and the emotion, but these things are not enough. A man is not saved through emotion and thought. A sinner falls at the Lord's feet because the speaker's spirit has released light through his speaking. As soon as our spirit gushes out, others are struck. This is the reason we need a released spirit to preach the gospel.

A coal miner was greatly used by the Lord in preaching the gospel. He wrote a book entitled *Seen and Heard* in which he described his experience with the gospel. We were deeply touched by this book. This brother was not an educated or gifted man; he was only an ordinary brother. But his absolute consecration to the Lord became the basis for the Lord to use him greatly. Do you know what was so special about him? He was a broken man. His spirit could be released easily. He started to preach at the age of twenty-three, when he first experienced salvation. In one meeting the word of a preacher kindled a burning desire within him to save souls. He asked to be allowed to speak. After he stood up, he was unable to say anything, even though his heart was burning with fire for lost souls. His tears came down like a torrent. In the end he could only utter one or two sentences. God's Spirit filled the meeting, and everyone was convicted of his own sin and waywardness. Here was a man who, in spite of his young age, was broken in the outer man. He did not have much to say, yet his spirit was released and men were saved. He led many people to salvation during his lifetime. When we read his biography, we sense that he was a man with a released spirit.

This is the way to preach the gospel. The way to preach the gospel is to release the spirit. When the hardness of the outer man is removed and the outer man is broken, the spirit is released. If the very sight of an unsaved person compels us to do something to save him, it means that our spirit is released. This is the basic issue. The preaching of the gospel has everything to do with the breaking of the outer man. When the outer man is broken, our spirit will be released and will touch others. It is our spirit that reaches others' spirits. It is God's Spirit that touches the darkened spirit of man. When this happens, a man is saved, and no reason can account for this change. However, when the outer man chokes the spirit, God does not have a way through us and the gospel will not be released. We always have to pay attention to the matter of the breaking of the outer man because all of our problems lie in the outer man. If we, the person, are not dealt with, it is useless for us to memorize more teachings. The only thing that will bring salvation to men is for our spirit to touch others' spirits. If our spirit touches others' spirits, they will fall on their face before God. If our spirit is discharged in a strong way, they will have no choice but to prostrate themselves before the Lord.

During these years God has been taking the way of recovery. God does not want to see a saved person wait for many years before he deals with his sins. He does not want to see him wait for many years before he consecrates himself to the Lord or answers the Lord's call to follow Him. The Lord is taking the way of recovery. The gospel has to be recovered, and the fruit of the gospel has to be recovered as well. As soon as a man is saved, he should be delivered from sin and should consecrate himself absolutely to the Lord. As soon as he is saved, he should break the power of mammon in him. He should be like the ones who were saved by the Lord in the Gospels and in Acts. If the gospel is indeed to be recovered, the preachers of the gospel must allow the Lord to cut a free way through them.

We believe that as the Lord takes the way of recovery, the gospel of grace will become one with the gospel of the kingdom. In the Gospels we see no separation between the gospel of the kingdom and the gospel of grace. Later, it seems as though those who heard the gospel of grace did not have a chance to hear the gospel of the kingdom. The gospel of grace seems to have been separated from the gospel of the kingdom. But the time will come when the gospel of grace will become one with the gospel of the kingdom once again. Those who receive the Lord will also give up everything for Him. Those who accept Him will also consecrate everything to Him. Men will no longer be saved in a poor way but in a strong and thorough way.

We have to humble ourselves before the Lord and say, "The gospel needs to be recovered, and the ones who preach the gospel also need to be recovered." In order for the gospel to reach men, we have to allow God to work through us. A greater power is needed for the preaching of the gospel. Even so, a greater price needs to be paid. If we expect both the gospel as well as the ones who preach the gospel to be recovered, we have to give everything to the Lord and say, "Lord, I give my all to You. I pray that You will find a way through me.

I pray that the church will also find a way through me. I do not want to hinder You or the church."

The Lord Jesus was never a limitation to God. He never limited God in any way. Throughout the past two thousand years God has been working in the church. The goal is for the church to eventually not be a limitation to Him either. Just as Christ was God's manifestation rather than His limitation, the church should be His manifestation rather than His limitation. God has been teaching, buffeting, stripping, and smiting His children continually. This is how He deals with the church. He will continue this work in the church until the church no longer is a limitation to Him but a manifestation of Him instead. Today we can only bow down our heads and say, "Lord! We are ashamed that we have delayed Your work. We have frustrated Your life, Your gospel, and Your power." Each one of us has to say to the Lord, "I give my all to You. I pray that You will have a way through me." If we want to see an absolute recovery of the gospel, we have to have an absolute consecration. It is foolish to only lament the fact that our gospel is not as powerful as that of the early church. We have to acknowledge that our consecration is not as absolute as the consecration of the early church. In order to recover the gospel, we have to recover the consecration; both have to be absolute and thorough. May the Lord find a way through us.

Chapter Six

BREAKING AND DISCIPLINE

CONSECRATION AND DISCIPLINE

In order for our outer man to be broken, we need to consecrate ourselves to the Lord. Consecration, however, does not take care of all the problems. It is only an expression of our intention to willingly give ourselves unconditionally, unreservedly, and unequivocally to God. We can consecrate ourselves to God in just a few minutes. This willingness to offer ourselves unreservedly to Him only constitutes the initial step in our spiritual journey. It does not mean that God has finished all of His work with this one step. Whether or not a man can be used by God does not depend on consecration alone. After consecration there is still the need of discipline from the Holy Spirit. This is very important, and whether or not we will become useful to God depends a great deal on this. The discipline of the Holy Spirit must be added to our consecration before we can become a useful vessel to the Lord. Without consecration, it often will be hard to go on with the discipline of the Holy Spirit. However, consecration alone cannot replace the Spirit's discipline. Therefore, we have to turn our attention to the matter of the Spirit's discipline.

In consecration we offer ourselves to God according to the light we have received. In disciplining us the Holy Spirit deals with us according to the light that He dispenses to us. We can only consecrate according to what we know. We can only consecrate according to what we can see with our spiritual eyes. In reality even we do not know how much is included in our consecration. The amount of light we have received is not infinite; our light is very limited. Even when we think that we have the greatest light, God's eyes still may find us in darkness. What we consecrate to God according to our perceived light will never satisfy His demand. In other words, God's demand is always higher than what we can offer. Our consecration cannot satisfy God's heart because our knowledge is limited and our light is limited. But the discipline of the Holy Spirit is altogether different; it evaluates our need in God's own light. It is not what we see, but what God sees. He knows that we have certain needs, and He operates through His Spirit in the environment for us to experience these things, the purpose of which is to break our outer man. Therefore, the disciplining work of the Holy Spirit goes far beyond our consecration. It is many times greater than our consecration. There is a big difference here.

The work of the Holy Spirit is based on the light of God. The Spirit works according to what God sees. Therefore, only the discipline of the Holy Spirit is thorough and complete. We often are ignorant in ourselves; we do not know what we need to go through. Even our wisest choices are full of errors. What we think we need often is not what we actually need according to God. What we see from our side may only be a tiny fraction of the whole picture. The Holy Spirit, however, orders things for us according to God's light. The discipline of the Holy Spirit far exceeds what our mind can fathom. We often are not prepared for a certain discipline, and we think that there is no need for it. When the Spirit's discipline does come upon us, we are taken by surprise. What the Spirit has ordered for us in the environment is not what we expected. Much discipline from the Holy Spirit comes without any warning from God. Suddenly we are struck with a heavy blow. We may think that we are living under God's light, but to God this light may be a very feeble flicker. He may not even consider it as light at all. The Holy Spirit, however, deals with us according to God's light. We think that we know our condition, but actually we do not. Only God knows us. From the time we accepted Him, He has been ordering our environment. Everything that He has ordered is for our greatest benefit because He knows us and He knows our needs.

The work of the Holy Spirit in us has a positive aspect and a negative aspect to it. There is a building-up aspect and a

tearing-down aspect. After we are regenerated, the Holy
Spirit lives in us, yet our outer man limits His freedom. This
is like a man wearing a pair of new shoes; the shoes are too
stiff and tight, and he finds it difficult to walk in them. The
outer man gives the inner man a difficult time. The inner
man cannot control the outer man. This is the reason that
God has been dealing with our outer man and breaking it
from the day we were saved. God does not deal with our
outer man according to our perceived need but according to
our need as He sees it. He finds out what is tenacious in us
and what is beyond the control of the inner man, and He
deals with us according to what He knows.

The Holy Spirit does not deal with our outer man by
strengthening our inner man. He does not deal with it by supplying our inner man with more grace. This does not mean
that the inner man does not need to be strengthened. It means
that God has a different way of dealing with the outer man.
The Holy Spirit diminishes our outer man by means of outward things. It is not too easy to tackle the outer man with the
inner man, because they are of different natures. It is hard
for the inner man to bruise or crush the outer man. The
nature of the outer man corresponds to the nature of outward
things; the outer man is easily affected by the outward things.
The outward things can crush, inflict pain, and bruise the
outer man much better than the inner man can. Therefore,
God deals with our outer man with outward things.

Matthew 10:29 says, "Are not two sparrows sold for an
assarion?" Luke 12:6 says, "Are not five sparrows sold for two
assaria?" One assarion buys two sparrows, and two assaria
buy five. This is cheap. The fifth one is a bonus; it is free. Yet,
"not one of them will fall to the earth apart from your Father"
(Matt. 10:29). The Bible also says, "Even the hairs of your
head are all numbered" (v. 30). Not only are all the hairs
counted; they are numbered. This leads us to realize that
everything that happens to a Christian is under God's ordering. No environment comes to us by accident. God wants us to
see that everything is under His sovereign arrangement.

God arranges all these things according to our need as
He sees it. He knows what is best for our inner man and how

best to break and dismantle our outer man. He knows that a certain thing will break our outer man, and He orders it to come upon us once, twice, and again and again. We have to see that all the things we have encountered during the past five or ten years have all been under God's ordering and are for our education. If we murmur against any person, we are indeed ignorant of God's hand. If we think that it was bouts of bad luck, we have no idea what the discipline of the Holy Spirit is. We have to remember that all the things that come upon us are measured by our God's hand. All these are for our good. We may not know to choose them, but God knows that they are for our good. I am not sure what misery we would have fallen into had it not been for such discipline from God. Such arrangements keep us pure; they preserve us in God's pathway. They are the best for us. God can give us nothing better. Many people cannot submit themselves. They murmur with their mouth and resent in their heart. This is indeed foolish. We have to remember that everything is measured to us by the Holy Spirit and is the best that it can be.

As soon as a person is saved, the Holy Spirit begins this work. But a period of time has to lapse before He can gain full liberty through this work. When does the Holy Spirit have the full liberty? It is when we consecrate ourselves. The day that a man is saved is the day that the Holy Spirit begins the disciplining work, and the day that he consecrates himself is the day that the Holy Spirit has the full freedom to perform such a work. After a man is saved and before he is consecrated, he still loves himself dearly and has little love for the Lord. One cannot say that the Holy Spirit is not disciplining him; He does order things to bring him to God and to break his outer man. But with an unconsecrated man, He does not have the full liberty to do this work. After a man is enlightened by God and has consecrated himself to God, the Holy Spirit will have the liberty to do His work. At a certain point, a man will feel that he can no longer live by himself or for himself. Under the feeble light that he apprehends, he will come to God and say, "I consecrate myself to You. Whether the outcome is death or life, I will consecrate myself to You."

When this happens, the Holy Spirit's work in him will be intensified. Consecration is important. Through consecration we allow the Holy Spirit to have the full and unconditional freedom to do His work. We should not be surprised when many things come upon us unexpectedly after we have consecrated ourselves. The only reason for such things to come upon us is that we have committed ourselves unconditionally to the Lord. We have said, "Lord, accomplish in me what is most profitable in Your sight!" Because we consecrated ourselves in this way, the Holy Spirit is free to do His work in us without concern for resistance on our part. Either we do not take the Lord's way at all, or if we do, we have to pay the utmost attention to the disciplining work of the Holy Spirit.

THE GREATEST MEANS OF RECEIVING GRACE

From the day a person is saved, God has been edifying him through the impartation of grace. A man can receive grace from God through many ways. We call these ways the means of receiving grace. For example, prayer is a means of receiving grace because we can go to God and receive grace through prayer. Listening to a message can also be a means of receiving grace because we can go to God and receive grace through listening. The expression *means of receiving grace,* or simply *means of grace,* is a good expression. The church has been using this expression for hundreds of years. We receive grace through means of grace. From the day we became a Christian, our daily life has been one in which we receive one means of grace after another. Our meetings, our listening to messages, our prayer, and many other things we do are means by which we obtain grace. Here we would like to point out one thing: The greatest means of receiving grace, one which we should never neglect, is the discipline of the Holy Spirit. The chief means of receiving grace in the Christian life is the discipline of the Holy Spirit. No other means of grace, such as prayer, Bible study, meeting together, listening to messages, waiting, meditation, or praise, can match this means of grace—the discipline of the Holy Spirit. Of all the means of grace that we receive from God, none is more important than this. The discipline of the Holy Spirit is the greatest means of receiving grace.

When we look back and examine our experience of the various means of grace, we will get an idea of how much we have gone on with God. If our spiritual progress has been through prayer, listening to messages, and reading the Bible alone, we have missed the chief means of receiving grace. All the things that come upon us every day in the family, in our school, in our work, or even on the street are arranged by the Holy Spirit for our highest good and profit. If we have not received profit from them and if we remain ignorant and closed to this greatest means of grace, we will suffer the greatest loss. The discipline of the Holy Spirit is too crucial; it is a Christian's main means of receiving grace throughout his life. Our reading of the Bible cannot replace the discipline of the Holy Spirit. Our prayer cannot replace the discipline of the Holy Spirit. Our meetings cannot replace the discipline of the Holy Spirit. No other means of grace can replace the discipline of the Holy Spirit. We need to pray, to study the Bible, to listen to messages, and to have all kinds of means of grace. They are all precious, but none of them can replace the discipline of the Holy Spirit. If we have not learned the proper lessons in the discipline of the Holy Spirit, we cannot be proper Christians and can never serve God. Listening to messages can nourish our inner being. Prayer can revive us inwardly. Reading God's Word can refresh us within. Helping others can release our spirit. However, if our outer man remains strong, others will encounter mixture when they encounter us; they will realize that we are not that pure. On the one hand, they will feel our zeal; on the other hand, they will sense our mixture. On the one hand, they will see that we do love the Lord; on the other hand, they also will know that we love ourselves. On the one hand, they can say that here is a precious brother; on the other hand, they have to say that here is a stubborn brother. The outer man is not yet broken. We are edified not only when we pray, listen to messages, and study the Bible. Our greatest edification comes when we are under the discipline of the Holy Spirit.

We need an absolute consecration on our side. But we can never assume that consecration can replace the discipline of the Holy Spirit. Consecration affords the Holy Spirit a chance to work on us freely. We should say, "Lord, I commit myself to Your hand. I allow You to work freely. Lord, give me what You think I need." If we yield to the arrangement of the Holy Spirit, we will reap the benefit. The very act of yielding will bring us benefit. But if we do not yield, instead arguing with God and walking according to our own will, we will end up taking the crooked path no matter what way we take. The basic issue is whether or not we can give ourselves to God unconditionally, unreservedly, and unequivocally for Him to deal with us freely. If we realize that all of God's arrangements are for our highest good, including those things that bring us embarrassment, and if we are willing to give ourselves to God in this way, we will find the Holy Spirit dealing with us in many things.

ALL KINDS OF DEALINGS

Some people are particularly bound by certain things. The Lord deals with them in those particular things. He deals with them item by item, including such minute details as their food and clothing. God will not let them go. How fine the Holy Spirit is! He does not neglect anything. We may love a certain thing without even realizing it ourselves. Yet God knows, and He will deal with us in a very detailed way. When all these things are taken away, we will be completely free. The Holy Spirit deals with many people by touching certain things. He goes after their cherished items relentlessly. Through such dealings, we begin to appreciate the way the Spirit attends to all the details. Even things that we have missed and forgotten are picked up by the Lord. He never forgets anything. God's work is perfect. He will not stop working until He reaches perfection. He will not be satisfied until He reaches that point. Sometimes God deals with us through men. He puts men around us whom we hate, envy, or despise and deals with us through them. He also puts lovable men around us to deal with us. Before we pass through the dealings, we have no realization of how filthy and impure we are.

After we pass through His dealings, we will see how impure we are. We think that we are totally given to the Lord. But after we pass through the discipline of the Holy Spirit, we will realize how much outward things affect us.

Sometimes God touches our thoughts. Our thoughts are confused, wild, self-motivated, and undisciplined. We think that we are clever, that we know everything, and that we can think of things that others cannot think of. Because of this, the Lord allows us to make mistakes and stumble again and again so that we would be wary of our own thoughts. If we find great grace in the Lord, we will shy away from our thoughts as much as we shy away from fire. As soon as the hand touches fire, it pulls back. In the same way as soon as we touch our thoughts, we turn back and tell ourselves, "This is not what I should think. I fear my own thoughts." Sometimes God deals with our emotions through ordering various circumstances for us. Some people are too strong in their emotions. When they are happy, they cannot stop rejoicing. When they are depressed, they cannot be comforted. Their whole life revolves around their emotions. If they are sad, no one can make them sing. If they are happy, no one can make them sober. Their happiness drives away their sobriety, and their sadness leads them into passivity. They are fully manipulated by their own emotions. Because they live in their emotions this way, they even justify their own emotions. For this reason God has to deal with their emotions through all kinds of circumstances. They have to be so dealt with that they dare not be sad or happy any longer; they can only live by God's grace and mercy, not by their own emotion.

The weakness of some people relates to their thoughts, while with others it relates to their emotions. Abnormal thoughts and emotions, however, are not common to everyone (though not a few have them). The biggest weakness and the most common one relates to the will. Because our will is untouched, our emotion becomes a problem to us. The root lies in the will. It is easy for us to say, "Not according to my will, but according to Your will." But when we go through our experiences, how many times do we truly own Him as Lord? The less a man knows himself, the easier it is for him to talk like this. The less a man is enlightened by God, the more he thinks that he will have no trouble obeying God. The quicker a man makes loud claims, the more it proves that he has never paid any price. Those whose words pretend intimacy with God are probably farthest away from Him. When one does not have the light, it is easy for him to claim intimacy with God. Actually such ones are far from God. A man must go through God's dealings before he will find out how stubborn and opinionated he is. He always believes in himself and considers his own opinions, feelings, methods, and views to be right. Paul found grace with God in many ways, the chief one of which, I believe, lies in his words in Philippians 3:3: "Have no confidence in the flesh." This means that he no longer trusted in his flesh. We also have to be led by God to realize that we dare not trust in our own judgment. God allows us to make mistakes again and again until we are forced to confess that we have been wrong in the past and that we will be wrong again in the future. We will acknowledge that we need the Lord's grace. The Lord often allows our judgment to bring us serious consequences. We make certain judgments, and they turn out to be wrong. We make other judgments, and they turn out to be wrong again, so terribly wrong that we cannot even salvage the loss. Time after time the Lord smites us, until a point is reached when as soon as we need to make a judgment, we will say, "I fear my own judgment as much as I fear hell fire. I am afraid that my judgment is flawed. I am afraid that my view and my methods are flawed. Lord, I am prone to mistakes. I am simply a man of mistakes! Lord, unless You grant me mercy and hold me by my hand and protect me with Your hand, I will fall into mistakes!" When we pray this way, our outer man will begin to crumble. We no longer will dare to trust in ourselves. We often make rash judgments; our views are too simplistic. But after a man is dealt with and broken by God time after time, and after he has passed through all kinds of failures, he will humble himself and say, "God, I dare not think, and I dare not decide." God deals with us in many ways through all kinds of things and people. This is the discipline of the Holy Spirit.

The discipline of the Holy Spirit is a lesson that will never slacken in us. Sometimes we lack the ministry of the word or other means of grace. But this means of receiving grace—the discipline of the Holy Spirit—is never lacking. The supply of the word can vary according to limitations in circumstances. But the discipline of the Holy Spirit is not limited by any circumstance. In fact, it becomes more manifest through limitations in the circumstance. Sometimes, we can say that we do not have the opportunity to listen to a message, but we can never say that we do not have the opportunity to obey the discipline of the Holy Spirit. We can say that we do not have the opportunity to receive the ministry of the word, but we cannot say that we do not have the opportunity to receive the teaching of the Holy Spirit. The Holy Spirit is arranging things every day and providing us with plenty of opportunities to learn our lessons.

If we can yield to God, the discipline of the Holy Spirit will be found to be a very fitting means for us, more so than the ministry of the word. We have to be clear about this way. We should never be mistaken to think that the supply of the word is the only means of receiving grace. Do not forget that the greatest means of receiving grace is the discipline of the Holy Spirit. It is the chiefest among all means of receiving grace. It is not available just to those who are educated, clever, and gifted but to those who are uneducated, dull, and short of gifts as well. The discipline of the Holy Spirit does not grant special favor to anyone. As long as a person is a child of God, he can commit himself unconditionally to God no matter who he is, and he can witness the discipline of the Holy Spirit. Through the discipline of the Holy Spirit, one learns many practical lessons. Some may think that it is good enough for them to have the ministry of the word, the grace of prayer, the fellowship with other believers, and many other means of grace. But they have to realize that no means of grace can replace the discipline of the Holy Spirit. Prayer cannot replace the discipline of the Holy Spirit, nor can the ministry of the word, the study of the Scriptures, or meditation. This is because we not only need the building up but also the tearing down. There are too many things in us that cannot go into eternity, and these must all be torn down.

THE CROSS IN PRACTICE

The cross is not merely a doctrine. It has to be carried out in practice. The cross has to be realized in us; all the things that belong to us have to be destroyed. As we are smitten once, twice, many times, there will come a time when spontaneously we will become sober; we will no longer be arrogant. The way is not through denying our arrogance when our memory reminds us of it. That kind of denial will disappear in five minutes. Only after a man passes through God's chastisement will his pride be forever stripped. A man may be proud at first, but after he is smitten by God once, twice, many times, he will begin to humble himself, and his arrogance will begin to erode away. No teaching, doctrine, or memorization will destroy the outer man. Only God's chastisement and the Spirit's discipline will destroy it. When a person is dealt with by God, spontaneously he will not dare to be proud. He does not have to force himself to remember this lesson. He does not act this way because he has heard a message a few days ago about it. He is not acting according to teaching. His pride has been knocked out, removed. He abhors his own methods and views them like fire; he is afraid of being burned. We live by God's grace, not by our memory. God has to smite us to the extent that we will be the same whether or not we remember to act that way. Such a work is reliable and lasting. When the Lord finishes such a work in us, we will not only receive grace and be strong in our inner being, but the outer man which was once a hindrance and frustration to the Lord's word, purpose, and presence will now be broken. Formerly, the outer man and the inner man could not be joined together. Now the outer man prostrates in fear and trembling; it has yielded itself to God and is no longer at odds with the inner man.

Every one of us needs to go through dealings from the Lord. In looking back, we find the Lord dealing with us item by item. He is continually breaking our outer shell and knocking down our outward independence, pride, and selfishness.

When we look back at all that has happened in the past, we have to acknowledge that everything the Lord has done is meaningful.

I hope that God's children would see the significance of the discipline of the Holy Spirit. God wants us to see that we are poor, that we have been going against Him, that we have failed, that we have lived in darkness, walked by ourselves, and been proud and arrogant for a long time. Now we know that the Lord's hand is on us to break us. Let us put ourselves in His hand unreservedly and unconditionally, praying that this breaking work will be accomplished in us. Brothers and sisters, the outer man must be broken! Do not try to save the outer man from being wrecked while hoping to build up the inner man. As we pay attention to the work of breaking, we will spontaneously witness the work of building.

CHAPTER SEVEN

SEPARATION AND REVELATION

God not only wants to break our outer man, but also to separate it from the inner man. He wants to dismantle our outer man so that our outer man does not become an encumbrance to the inner man. He wants our spirit and our soul, that is, our inner man and our outer man, to be separated from each other.

A MIXED SPIRIT

A problem among God's children is the mixture of the soul with the spirit. Whenever their spirit is released, their soul is released as well. It is hard to find a person whose spirit is pure. With many people this purity is lacking. It is this mixture that disqualifies them from being used by God. The first qualification in the work is a purity of the spirit, not a measure of power. Many people hope to have great power, yet they pay no attention to purity in the spirit. Although they have the power to build, they are short in purity. As a result their work is bound for destruction. On the one hand, they build with power. On the other hand, they destroy with their impurity. They demonstrate God's power, yet at the same time their spirit is a mixed spirit.

Some people think that as long as they receive power from God, everything that they have will be sublimated and be taken up by God for His service. But this will never happen. Whatever belongs to the outer man will forever belong to the outer man. The more we know God, the more we will treasure purity over power. We cherish this purity. This purity is different from spiritual power, and it is free from any contamination of the outer man. If a man has never experienced any dealing in his outer man, it is impossible to expect the power that issues from him to be pure. He cannot assume that just because he has spiritual power and has produced some results in his work that he is free to mix his self with his spirit. If he does this, he will become a problem. This, in fact, is a sin.

Many young brothers and sisters know that the gospel is the power of God. But when they preach the gospel, they add in their own cleverness, frivolity, jokes, and personal feelings. Others can sense God's power with them, but at the same time they also sense the self. The preachers themselves may not feel anything, but the pure ones immediately will sense the presence of mixture. We often are zealous for God's work outwardly, yet in reality we mix in our own preferences. We often are doing God's will outwardly, but actually it is only a coincidence that God's will matches our will. Many so-called wills of God are mixed up with man's preferences! Much zeal is mixed up with man's sentiment! Many stout testimonies for God are mixed up with man's stubborn disposition!

Our greatest problem is our mixture. Hence, God has to work on us to break our outer man as well as to remove our mixture. God is breaking us step by step so that our outer man will no longer be whole. After our outer man is battered once, ten, twenty times, we will be broken and our hard outer shell before God will be gone. But what should we do with the mixture of the outer man in our spirit? This requires another work—the work of purging. This work is carried out not only through the discipline of the Spirit, but also through the revelation of the Spirit. The way to purge mixture is different from the way to break the outer man. The way to purge mixture is often through revelation. Therefore, we find God dealing with us in two ways. One is the breaking of the outer man, and the other is the separation of the outer man from the spirit. One comes through the discipline of the Holy Spirit, and the other is the result of the revelation of the Holy Spirit.

THE NEED OF BREAKING AND SEPARATION

Breaking and separation are our two different needs. Yet there is a strong relationship between the two, and it is impossible to disassociate the two altogether. The outer man needs to be broken before the spirit can be released. But when the spirit is released, it must not be mixed with the sentiments and characteristics of the outer man. It must not carry any element that comes from man. This is not merely a matter of the release of the spirit, but a matter of the purity and quality of the spirit. Many times when a brother stands up to speak, on the one hand, we feel the spirit and the presence of God. However, on the other hand, we touch his self in his words; we touch his conspicuous spot. His spirit is not pure. He can give us a cause for praise, yet at the same time be a source of pain. The issue is not whether the spirit is released, but whether the spirit is pure.

If a man has never been enlightened by God or judged by Him in a deep way, thereby gaining a knowledge of his outer man, the release of his spirit naturally will be accompanied by his outer man. When many people speak, we can sense the release of their very person. They release God, but the release of their spirit is accompanied by their own uncondemned self because many things in them have never passed through judgment. When we contact others, they are primarily touched by our most conspicuous and outstanding elements. If our outer man is not condemned, what will be exposed as soon as we come in contact with others will be the most conspicuous element of the outer man. No one can hide this. Many people who are not even spiritual in their own room expect to be spiritual when they stand on the platform. This is impossible. Many people lose their spirituality as soon as their memory fails to remind them. Their spirituality is sustained by their memory. But this is an impossible proposition. We should not think, "I will remember to muzzle myself today because I have to give a message; I have to work." Our memory is not our salvation. We cannot be saved by our memory. Whatever kind of person we are will be exposed as soon as we open our mouth. No matter how hard a person tries to pretend, act, or cover up himself, his spirit comes out as soon as he opens his mouth. Whatever kind of spirit we have and whatever mixture there is in our spirit will be obvious to everyone as soon as we open our mouth. In spiritual matters, there is no way to pretend.

If we want to experience deliverance from God, this deliverance must be fundamental, not fragmentary. God has to work in us to deal with our strong point, and He has to break it. Only then will our spirit be released without mixture being imparted to others. If we have never been touched by God in a fundamental way, we may act somewhat spiritual when we remember to do it, but we will manifest the self once our memory slips. Actually, in both cases, whether we remember or we forget, the spirit that we release is the same, and the things that are carried by the spirit are the same.

The problem of mixture is the biggest problem among workers. We often touch life in the brothers, but also touch death. We touch God in the brothers, but also touch their self. We touch a spirit of meekness, but also touch a stubborn self. We find the Holy Spirit in them, but also find the flesh in them. When they stand up to speak, others sense a mixed spirit, an impure spirit. If God intends for us to serve Him in the ministry of the word and if we have to speak for God, we have to ask for grace. We have to say, "God, work in me. Break my outer man, tear it down, and separate it from the inner man." If we have not experienced this deliverance, we will express our outer man subconsciously every time we open our mouth. There is no way for us to hide it. As soon as the word goes out, the spirit goes out as well. We are the kind of person we are; we cannot pretend. If we want to be used by God, our spirit must be released, and this spirit must be pure. In order for us to be pure, our outer man must be destroyed. If our outer man is not destroyed, we will carry our own cargo with us when we serve as ministers of the word. The Lord's name will suffer loss, not on account of our lack of life, but on account of our mixture. The Lord's name will suffer, and the church will suffer as well.

We have spoken of the discipline of the Holy Spirit. Now we would like to speak on the revelation of the Holy Spirit. It is possible for the discipline of the Spirit to come before the revelation of the Spirit, and it is possible for the order to be reversed. We can make a distinction in sequence, but when the Holy Spirit works, He does not necessarily do one thing first and then the other. In our experience there is no set order of events. Some people experience discipline first. Other people experience revelation first. Everyone's experience is different. Some receive the discipline of the Spirit first, then the revelation of the Spirit, and then more discipline. Others receive the revelation of the Spirit first, then discipline, and then more revelation. However, among God's children there is always more discipline of the Holy Spirit than revelation of the Holy Spirit. Here we are speaking about experience, not doctrine. With many people, discipline occurs more often than revelation. In short, the soul and the spirit have to be separated. The inner man must be separated from the outer man. The outer man must be broken, pulverized, and completely separated from the inner man. Only then will our spirit be free and pure.

HOW TO BE SEPARATED

Hebrews 4:12-13 says, "For the word of God is living and operative and sharper than any two-edged sword, and piercing even to the dividing of soul and spirit and of joints and marrow, and able to discern the thoughts and intentions of the heart. And there is no creature that is not manifest before Him, but all things are naked and laid bare to the eyes of Him to whom we are to give our account." *Word* in verse 12 is *logos* in Greek. *Account* in verse 13 is also *logos* in Greek. This carries the meaning of judgment. The last part of verse 13 can be translated as "all things are naked and laid bare to the eyes of Him who judges us" or "all things are naked and laid bare to the eyes of the Lord; the Lord is our Judge."

The first thing we have to realize is that the Bible tells us that God's word is living. If we really touch God's word, it will be living to us. If we do not sense the livingness of God's word, it proves that we have not touched God's word. Some people have read through all the words of the Bible. But they have not touched God's word. Only to the extent that we have touched something living can we claim that we have touched God's word.

John 3:16 says, "For God so loved the world that He gave His only begotten Son, that every one who believes into Him would not perish, but would have eternal life." One person hears this word and kneels down, praying, "Lord, I thank and praise You because You love me and save me." This is a person who has touched God's word, because His word has become living to him. Another man sitting right next to him may hear the same word. The sound may be the same, but he only is hearing the sound; he does not hear God's word. There is no living response within him when he hears the word. God's word is living. If a man hears the word and does not become living, he has not heard the word. God uses His own word, and this word is living.

God's word is not only living, but operative. *Living* refers to its nature, and *operative* refers to the works which it accomplishes in man according to God's will. God's word does not pass away lightly. It always results in something. It produces results. God's word does not come to us void. It operates to produce results in man.

God's word is living and operative. What does this word do to man? It pierces and divides. God's word is sharp, even "sharper than any two-edged sword." It pierces "even to the dividing of soul and spirit and of joints and marrow." Here is a contrast. On the one side, we have a two-edged sword versus the joints and marrow. On the other side, we have God's word versus the soul and the spirit. The joints and marrow are the deepest parts of man. To divide the joints is to divide the bone outwardly. To divide the marrow is to divide the bone inwardly. A two-edged sword can divide a bone outwardly and inwardly. Physically, a two-edged sword can do this to our body. But there are two things which are harder to divide than the joints and the marrow: the soul and the spirit. A sharp, two-edged sword can divide joints and marrow, but it cannot divide soul and spirit. It cannot tell us what the soul is and what the spirit is. It cannot show us what is of the soul and what is of the spirit. But the Bible says that one thing, which is sharper than any two-edged sword, can divide the soul and the spirit. It is the word of God. God's word is living, and God's word is operative. It can pierce and divide. What it pierces is not the joints and what it divides is not the marrow. It pierces to the dividing of the soul and the spirit. It can separate the soul from the spirit.

Some may say, "I do not feel that God's word can do anything. I have been listening to God's word for a long time, and I have accepted His revelation. But I have not received anything special. I do not know what it means to pierce and to divide. I know that God's word pierces even to the dividing of soul and spirit. But in my experience I do not know what it means to pierce and to divide."

The Bible answers this concern. In the first part of the verse it says, "Piercing even to the dividing of soul and spirit and of joints and marrow." What does it mean to pierce to the dividing of soul and spirit? The next part of the verse says, "And able to discern the thoughts and intentions of the heart." *Thoughts* are what we think in our heart, and *intentions* are our motives and purpose. God's word can discern what we think in our heart as well as our motives.

We often concede that something is of our outer man, that it is of the soul, of the flesh, and is fleshly. We concede that it is something that originates from ourselves. Yet even as we are saying this, we do not see this matter in actuality. When God grants us mercy and enlightens us, He will speak to us in a serious and sober way, as if to say, "This is it! This is the self that you have been talking about for a long time. This is your self! You have been talking so glibly and lightheartedly about the flesh. This is it! This is what I hate. This is what I abhor." When we do not see the flesh, we speak about it jokingly. When we are under the light, we will fall on our face and confess: "This is it! The flesh that I was speaking of is this very thing!" The dividing of the soul and the spirit is not a division in knowledge. It occurs when God's word comes to us and reveals the thoughts and intentions of our heart. The dividing of the soul and the spirit happens when, under God's shining, we see that our thoughts, our mind, and our actions are all of the flesh and that our motives are all for the self.

Suppose two sinners are before us. Both are sinners, but they are not the same. One is a sinner with knowledge. He comes to the meeting and hears many teachings. He knows that man is a sinner, and that he is a sinner by virtue of this and that fact. The preacher is lucid in his preaching, and our friend has picked up much knowledge. He confesses that he is a sinner. Yet in talking about himself being a sinner, he is very jovial and unconcerned. The other man hears the same thing, but God's light is upon him, and he falls on his face and says, "My goodness, this is me! I am a sinner!" He hears God's word telling him that he is a sinner, and he sees that he is a sinner. He condemns himself and falls on his face. This enlightened one prostrates himself on the floor and confesses his sins; he receives God's salvation. The other one who jokes about being a sinner does not see anything, and he is not saved.

Today we have heard that the outer man is a serious problem and that the fleshly man must be broken. If we speak about this subject lightly as if it is a subject for conversation, it will do us no good. If we receive God's mercy to see the light, we will say, "Lord! Today I know myself. I now know what is my outer man." When God's light shines on us, we will see what the outer man is, and we will fall down and not be able to rise again. We immediately will see that we are that very person. We say that we love the Lord, but when God's light shines on us, we will see that we did not love the Lord at all but instead only loved ourselves. When the light comes, it divides. The mind does not divide us. Doctrines do not divide us. God's light divides us. We boast of our zeal, but God's light will reveal this zeal as nothing but activities of the flesh. We preach the gospel and think that we love sinners, but when light comes, we will see that our preaching of the gospel was the result of our restlessness and talkativeness; it was only our natural inclination. When light comes, the motive and thoughts in our heart are exposed. We think that our thoughts and intentions are of the Lord, but when light comes, everything is exposed, and we will find that these were all of ourselves, not of the Lord at all. Once the light comes we will see, and when we see, we will fall at God's feet. Many things which we think are of the Lord will be found to be of ourselves. We foolishly claim that such and such is for the Lord, but when the light comes, we will realize how little of what we have done was for the Lord. Most of the things were done for ourselves.

We think that many works have been done by the Lord. Actually they all have been done by us. We boast that many messages that we preach are from the Lord. But when God's light shines on us, we will find that very little of what we have said were words given by the Lord. Perhaps there were no such words at all. We think that many works are commissioned by the Lord, but when the light breaks from heaven, we will see that all the works we have done were merely activities of the flesh. This revelation of our true state of affairs and the confrontation of reality become light to us. Then we will realize how much of what we have is of ourselves, of the soul, and how much is of the Lord and of the spirit. As soon as the light shines, the soul is divided from the spirit, and there is the discerning of the thoughts and intentions of the heart.

We cannot make this matter clear with doctrines. If we try to discern doctrinally what is of the self, what is of the Lord, what is of the flesh, what is of the Holy Spirit, what is of the Lord's grace, what is of the outer man, and what is of the inner man, we can spell out a long list and can even memorize the list, but we will still be in darkness. We will still do the same things. We will still be unable to get rid of the outer man. The things will still be with us, and we will still not be able to free ourselves from them. We can say that the flesh is wrong. We can jokingly point out that this is the flesh and that is the flesh, but this will not save us. Deliverance does not come this way; it comes from God's light. As soon as God's light shines on us, we will realize that even our rejection of the flesh is an act of the flesh. Even our criticism of the flesh is a word of the flesh. The Lord will discern the thoughts and the intentions of our heart. We will see the real condition of the thoughts and intentions of our hearts, and we will bow down and say, "Lord! Now I know that these things belong to the outer man." Brothers and sisters, only this light will separate our outer man from our inner man. The separation of the outer man does not come from denial. We cannot grit our teeth and say that we reject it. Our rejection is unreliable. Our confession is unclean. Even the tears of our confession have to be washed by the blood. We foolishly think that we possess what we know in our mind. But God does not see things this way.

God says that His word is living and operative. His word is sharper than anything else. When this word comes to us, the soul and the spirit are divided, even as a two-edged sword divides the joints and the marrow. It divides us by exposing the thoughts and intentions of the heart. Not many of us know our heart! Brothers and sisters, only those who are under the light know their own heart. Those who are not under the light never know their own heart. There is no exception to this! We do not know our heart at all. Only when God's word comes to us will we see that we have been only for ourselves. We live for our own satisfaction, our own glory, our own pursuit, our own position, and our own edification. Brothers and sisters, when the self is exposed and made manifest by the light, we will fall on our faces before God.

WHAT IS A REVELATION?

Hebrews 4:13 continues, saying, "And there is no creature that is not manifest before Him, but all things are naked and laid bare to the eyes of Him to whom we are to give our account." Here the Lord shows us the standard by which He enlightens us and discerns our thoughts and intentions. What constitutes a revelation of the Holy Spirit? To what extent do our eyes have to be opened before we can say that we have a revelation? This is what verse 13 tells us. Putting it in one sentence, the standard of light is the standard of God. Revelation means that we see things according to God's standard. All things are naked and laid bare before Him, and nothing is hidden from Him. Hiding something only hides it from our eyes; nothing can be hidden from the Lord's eyes. Revelation is God opening our eyes to see our intentions and the deepest thoughts in our being as God sees them. Just as we are naked and laid bare before Him, we are naked and laid bare before ourselves after we receive revelation. Just as we are manifest before God, we are manifest before ourselves after we receive revelation. This is revelation. Revelation is seeing what the Lord sees.

If God is merciful to us and grants us a little revelation, if we see a little of ourselves as God sees us, and if He reveals to us a little of what we are like, we will immediately fall on our face before the Lord. We will not have to force ourselves to be humble; we will fall by ourselves. Those who are in the light cannot be proud even if they want to. Only those who are in darkness are proud. A man is arrogant because he does not have God's light. All those who are in the light and in revelation surely will fall on their faces.

How do we know what is spiritual and what is soulish, what is from the inner man and what is from the outer man? It is hard to clarify this matter by means of doctrine. But if we have revelation, we will find this question simple to answer. As soon as God exposes our thoughts and shows us the intentions of our heart, our soul will be separated from our spirit. Whenever we are able to discern the thoughts and intentions of our heart, we are able to divide our soul from our spirit.

If we want to be useful, sooner or later we have to allow this light to shine upon us. Only when this light comes to us will we be under the Lord's judgment. When we are judged, we will be able to lift up our head and say, "God, I am totally unreliable. Even when I am rebuking myself, I am not trustworthy. Even while I am confessing my sins, I am still ignorant of what I am confessing. I can only know through the light." Before we receive light, we may say that we are sinners, but we do not have the sense of being a sinner. We say that we hate ourselves, but we do not have the feeling that we are actually hating ourselves. We say that we are denying ourselves, but we do not have the feeling that we are denying ourselves. This will only come through the Lord's shining. As soon as the light shines, our true self will be exposed. We will find that all our lives we have been loving ourselves, not the Lord. We have been deceiving ourselves and deceiving the Lord. We did not love the Lord at all. Light will show us the kind of persons we are and the kind of things we did before. From that day onward, we will know what is of the spirit and what is of the soul. We will know that many things were of ourselves. A man can only say that he knows after he has been judged by the light. If he is not judged by the light, he will not be what he claims to be even if he tries to imitate. Only as God shines a great light upon us can we say, "This is my soul." The judgment that comes with the light will distinguish the inner man from the outer man. When the inner man and the outer man are distinguished from one another, then our soul and spirit will be divided. The Lord does a kind of one-time shining in us with His unprecedented, great light. It may happen while we are listening to a message. It may happen while we are praying, fellowshipping with other brothers, or walking along the road. The unprecedented light shines, and we discover ourselves. Once we are placed under this great light, we will discover how little of what we have done in our lifetime has been of the Lord. It always has been ourselves. We have been the ones who have been acting, busily and zealously working, speaking, helping the brothers and sisters, and preaching the gospel. When the light shines on us, we will realize how pervasive our presence is, how we have extended ourselves into everything, and what our self encompasses.

The self that was previously hidden now will be exposed. The self that was removed from our consciousness now will be clearly felt. Everything will be clear, and we will realize that the self actually involves so much, including activities so numerous. We thought that many things were done in the name of the Lord. Now we will see that in essence they are all of ourselves. Once we see this, we will spontaneously condemn the outer man. The things that we see under the light will be condemned by us when they surface again. What we have seen under the light will be rejected by us again when things, words, or intentions of a similar nature arise a second time; we immediately will see that what we are faced with is the same thing that we were trying to deal with the first time. Anything that has passed through the judgment of light once will be judged again as soon as a little seed sprouts forth. After we have received this shining we will be able to divide the soul from the spirit. Before this shining, all we had were doctrines, and we spoke like a sinner glibly talking about his own sin. If we do not have the light, even our effort to deal with ourselves is useless. The only kind of dealing that is useful is the dealing under the light. When we live before the Lord in this way, our spirit will be released. We will become pure, and the Lord will not have any trouble using us.

The dividing of the soul and the spirit comes from the shining. What is the shining? May the Lord be merciful to us to show us what the shining is. Shining is seeing what God sees. What does God see? He sees what we do not see. What do we not see? We do not see the things that are of ourselves, the things that we think are of God but which are not. Light shows us how much of what we thought was of God is actually of ourselves. It shows us how much of what we thought was good is actually not good, how much of what we thought was right is actually wrong, how much of what we thought was spiritual is actually soulish, and how much of what we thought was of God is actually of ourselves. Then we will say, "Lord! Now I know myself. I am a blind man. I have been blind for twenty or thirty years, yet I have not realized it. I did not see what You have seen."

This seeing will take away what we have. Our seeing is the dealing. Do not think that seeing is one thing and dealing another thing. God's word is operative. Once His word shines on us, our outer man is gone. We do not hear God's word and then gradually experience the dealing afterwards. We do not see something through God's light and then deal with what we have seen afterwards. We do not have seeing as one step and dealing as another. The shining is the removing; both happen at the same time. As soon as the light shines, the flesh dies. No flesh survives when it is exposed to the light. When a man sees light, he does not have to humble himself; he will fall on his face immediately. Under the light his flesh will wilt away. Brothers and sisters, this is what it means to be operative. God's word is living and operative. This does not mean that God speaks, and then we make it operative. The word itself is operative in us.

May the Lord open our eyes to see these two things. On the one hand, we have the discipline of the Holy Spirit. On the other hand, we have revelation. These two things combined together will deal with our outer man. May the Lord be gracious to us so that we will put ourselves under His light, and may this light shine on us so that we will prostrate ourselves and say to the Lord, "I am indeed foolish and blind. I have been so foolish and blind that for years I have taken what is of myself to be of You. Lord, be merciful to me!"

Chapter Eight

IMPRESSION AND
THE CONDITION OF THE SPIRIT

BREAKING AND IMPRESSION

Whether or not we can be a worker of the Lord depends not on what we say or do but on what comes out of us. If we say and do one thing, yet what comes out of us is another thing, others will not receive help. What comes out of us is a very crucial matter.

Sometimes we say that we have a good impression of a certain person, or that we have a bad impression of another person. Where does this impression come from? The impression does not come from a person's words. If it does, then we would say that a person is good if his words are good and that he is bad if his words are bad; there would not be the need to talk about impression at all. Yet in reality there is something inexplicable which gives us certain impressions. The impressions that we receive of a person are something apart from his words and deeds. As he is speaking or acting, something else comes out of his being which impresses us with an impression.

What generates an impression in others is the strongest spots we have in ourselves. If our thoughts have never been broken and are lawless and wild, when we meet the brothers and sisters, they spontaneously will touch our thoughts. This will be all that impresses them. We may possess an abnormal emotion; it may be exceptionally warm or cold. If our emotion has never been broken by the Lord, it will spontaneously come out of us when we contact others. The impression others will receive will be of our emotion. Our strong spot will be what comes out of us, and it will be the impression that others receive. We can control our words and our actions, but we cannot control what flows out of us. Whatever we have will flow out of us spontaneously.

Second Kings 4 gives us the account of the Shunammite woman's reception of Elisha. The Bible says that "one day Elisha was passing through Shunem; and there was a wealthy woman there, who compelled him to have a meal. So whenever he passed through, he would turn aside and have a meal there. And she said to her husband, Now I know that this man who continually passes through unto us is a holy man of God" (vv. 8-9). Elisha passed through Shunem. He did not give one message or perform one miracle. Every time he passed through, he turned aside and had a meal there. The woman identified him as a man of God by the way he took his meal. This was the impression that Elisha gave to others.

Today we have to ask ourselves, "What is the impression that we give to others? What is the thing that comes out of us?" We have spoken repeatedly that the outer man must be broken. If the outer man is not broken, the impression that others receive from us will be nothing but the outer man. Every time we contact others, we may give them an unpleasant feeling that we are self-loving, stubborn, and proud. Or we may give them an impression that we are clever and extremely eloquent. Perhaps we give others a so-called good impression. But does this impression satisfy God? Does it meet the church's need? God is not satisfied, and the church has no need of our so-called good impressions.

Brothers, God requires that our spirit be released, and the church also requires that our spirit be released. We have a very great and crucial need: Our outer man must be broken. If the outer man is not broken, our spirit will not be released, and the impression we give to others will not be an impression of the spirit.

A brother once was speaking on the subject of the Holy Spirit, but all his words, attitude, and stories exposed him as a man full of the self. While others were listening, they were uncomfortable. The Holy Spirit was in his mouth, but the self was in his being. His words were on the Holy Spirit, but the impression he gave to others was of his self. What purpose does this serve? We must not pay attention to doctrines alone. The important thing is what comes out of us. If what comes out of us is the self, others will only touch the self. Even though our subject may be wonderful and our message excellent, what good will it serve? God has no intention for us to make progress in doctrine alone. He has to deal with the person. If our person is not dealt with, we will be of little use to God's work. We will only be able to give others spiritual teachings; we will not be able to give others spiritual impressions. It is a great pity if our teachings are spiritual but the impressions we give to others are of the self! This is the reason we repeatedly have spoken of the need for God to break our outer man.

Time after time, God has been arranging our circumstances to break our strong spot. It may be so strong that one blow is not enough to take it away. Therefore, a second blow comes. If our strong spot is still unyielding, a third blow will come. God will not let us go. He has to break our strong spot. He will never stop His work.

What the Holy Spirit accomplishes in us through His disciplining work is different from what we receive through ordinary preaching. In receiving a message, we generally understand the doctrine in our mind and then wait for months and even years before God leads us into the truth subjectively. We receive the message, and then we enter into the truth. But the discipline of the Holy Spirit works differently. It is characterized by the fact that the instant we see the truth, we receive the content of that truth itself. These two things occur at the same time. We do not see the doctrine and then receive the content later. We are foolish men; we understand doctrines quickly, but we learn from the discipline slowly. We can remember many teachings after hearing them once. Yet the discipline of the Holy Spirit may come to us ten times, and we still may be bewildered and astonished as to what we are being disciplined for. If the Lord cannot break us with one blow, He will do it again and again. As we experience the discipline of the Holy Spirit once, twice, ten times, or even a hundred times, the Lord will wrought something into us, and in that same moment we will see the truth. The moment we see the truth is the moment we acquire the thing itself. Hence, the discipline of the Holy Spirit equals both the breaking down and the building up of the Holy Spirit. This is the work of the Holy Spirit. After a man passes through the Spirit's discipline, he will be edified as well as see the truth; he will be built up as well as torn down. When he has experienced so much discipline from the Holy Spirit, he will see and touch something real before the Lord, and he will say, "Thank the Lord. Now I know that the Lord has used the past five or ten years to deal with me just for the purpose of getting rid of this one thing." Thank the Lord that He removes our obstacles through repeated dealings.

SHINING AND KILLING

Shining is another work of the Holy Spirit. The Spirit deals with our outer man by these two means: discipline and shining. Sometimes He works by both means simultaneously and at other times consecutively. Sometimes, the Holy Spirit disciplines us through the environment to knock out our strong spots. At other times, He grants us special grace by enlightening us in a special way. We must be clear that the flesh can only take shelter in darkness. When darkness is gone, the flesh has no place to hide. Many acts of the flesh remain because we do not know them as the flesh. As soon as light comes and we see them as the flesh, we become fearful to act the way we have before.

When the church is rich, when God's word is released, when the ministry of the word is strong, and when prophesying is common, light is frequent and prevailing. Once light shines, we realize what pride is. We begin to know the very thing that we have been talking about in the past. When we spoke of pride previously, it was something we boasted of. But when we see pride under the light, we can only exclaim, "My goodness! This is pride. Now I know that pride is so evil and filthy!" The pride that we see under the light of revelation is completely different from the pride that we speak of with our mouth. The pride that we so glibly speak of does not appear loathsome and filthy to us. Even while we are speaking about it, we have very little feeling. But when we are under the light, everything becomes different. Light exposes our true condition. The self that we see today is thousands of times more evil and filthy than the self that we spoke of in the past. Under such circumstances, our pride, self, and flesh will wilt away. They will be removed and no longer survive.

The wonderful thing is that whatever we see under the light is killed by the light. The seeing and the killing do not happen consecutively. We do not see our shortcomings and then remove them gradually years later. When we see our shortcomings under the shining, the shortcomings are finished immediately; they are killed immediately. Light kills; this is the most wonderful thing about the Christian experience. As the Holy Spirit enlightens us, we are dealt with. Therefore, revelation comprises seeing as well as killing. Through seeing, the flesh withers away. Revelation is God's way of operation. In fact, revelation is God's operation itself. As soon as light reveals, it kills. When light shines, we see, and our seeing kills everything. Once we see how filthy and evil something is and see the Lord's condemnation of it, it can no longer survive.

The greatest thing in the Christian experience is the killing that comes from light. Paul did not receive a shining and then hasten to kneel beside the road; the very instant he was enlightened, he fell down. Prior to that, he was able to plan for everything, and he was confident about everything. However, his first reaction when the light came was to fall down. He became foolish and ignorant. Light brought him down. We should take note that these two things happen as one step, not two steps. It does not happen the way we think. God does not shine on us and make us understand, and then we carry out what He has shown us. God does not enlighten us concerning our shortcomings, and then we begin to change these shortcomings. No, God does not work this way. He shows us how evil, filthy, and short we are, and as soon as we see this, we exclaim, "My! What a filthy and evil man I am!" As soon as God shows us our true condition, we fall. We wither away and are not able to stand up any longer. Once a proud man is enlightened, he is no longer able to be proud even if he tries. Once we have seen our true condition under God's light and once we have seen what our pride is, the impression will never leave us. Something will remain in us that will give us pain, that will give us the feeling that we are useless, and we will no longer be able to be proud.

When God shines on us, it is a time for believing and prostrating ourselves, not the time for petitioning. Many brothers and sisters busy themselves in prayer when God is speaking to them. As a result they do not see any light. The principle that brought us our initial salvation holds true for all subsequent works of God. At the time we were enlightened for our salvation, we did only one thing: We knelt down and prayed, "Lord, I accept You as my Savior." Following this, something happened. If a man prays after he hears the gospel, "Lord, I beg that You would be my Savior," he may pray the same prayer for a few days without feeling that the Lord has saved him. As soon as the Lord shines on us, we have to fall under His light and say, "Lord, I accept Your judgment. I accept Your view." If we do this, God will give us more light and will show us how filthy we are.

The day that God shines His light on us, many things will change before our eyes. We thought that we had done many things in the name of the Lord and for love's sake. Now the picture changes. We discover that hidden beneath our noblest goals are base and ugly motives. We thought that we were absolutely for God. Now we discover that we are full of plans for ourselves. In fact we are so full of these things that we can only fall on our faces. Man's self creeps into every nook and cranny; it even tries to usurp God's glory. "Is there anything that man cannot do?" Under God's shining, we find out the kind of person we are. As soon as God's revelation comes, our condition is exposed and laid bare. He exposes us, and we see ourselves. Previously, only the Lord knew us. We were naked and laid bare before Him, but not before ourselves; we still did not know ourselves. But when God exposes all of the thoughts and intentions of the heart to us, we become naked not only before Him, but before ourselves as well. When we are naked and laid bare before ourselves, we no longer dare to lift up our heads. Before we are exposed, we do not know ourselves, and we can easily get by. But when we see ourselves under God's light, we are so ashamed that no place is good enough for us to hide ourselves. Now we know what kind of person we are! Now we know the kind of boasts we made! We thought we were better than others. Now we know the kind of persons we are! We cannot find more fitting terms before the Lord to describe ourselves; we can only say that we are filthy and evil. We admit that our eyes have been blind for years, that they have seen nothing. The more we see our filth, the more ashamed we become. It seems as if all the shame of the whole world is upon us. We prostrate before the Lord and repent, saying, "I repent of myself. I hate myself. I admit that I am an incurable man."

This shining, repentance, shame, loathing, and prostration will shake off what we have been unable to shake off all these years. Man's salvation comes from this instant enlightening. The seeing and removing are one work; the two are joined together. As the Lord shines, He saves. The shining is the saving, and the seeing is the deliverance. We need this kind of seeing before the Lord. Only this kind of shining will remove our pride, and only this light will stop our fleshly activities and break our outer shell.

A COMPARISON BETWEEN
DISCIPLINE AND REVELATION

We have these two main things before us—the Spirit's discipline and God's shining, or we can say the Spirit's revelation. Let us make a comparison of the two things. The discipline of the Holy Spirit is generally a slow process. It comes to us slowly, little by little. Sometimes it takes a few years for Him to deal with us concerning a certain thing. Moreover, this discipline does not come necessarily through the ministry of the word. Many times there is no ministry of the word, yet the Spirit still exercises His discipline. But the revelation of the Holy Spirit is different. Often it comes quickly, maybe in days or even in minutes. God's light may shine on a man for a few minutes or a few days. Under this light he sees that he is finished, that he is absolutely useless, and that all of his former boasts are now his shame. Such revelation of the Holy Spirit often comes through the ministry of the word. This is the reason the revelation of the Holy

Spirit occurs more frequently when the church is strong and the ministry of the word abundant. But even when there is no ministry of the word, and consequently little revelation from the Spirit, no one can remain in the Lord's presence while still preserving his outer man. The word and the revelation may be lacking, but there is still the discipline of the Holy Spirit. Even if a person has not come into contact with any other believer for years, the Holy Spirit still performs His disciplining work on him, and a man can still learn and touch something high before the Lord. Some do not have the ministry of the word because the church is weak. Some even think that they have lost the discipline of the Spirit through their own foolishness. This does not mean that there is no longer any discipline of the Holy Spirit. Rather, it means that the Holy Spirit has been disciplining for years without producing anything or arriving at any result. The Lord may strike once, and we may not know what it means. He may strike again, and we still may not know what it means. He may strike for ten years, while we act like a mule without reason, unaware of His intentions. This is a pity. Discipline never falls short in us; what falls short is our vision of the Lord's hand.

The Lord often chastises us, but we turn our attention to men and take the wrong track. Our attitude before the Lord should be as the psalmist said, "I did not open my mouth; for You have done this" (Psa. 39:9). We have to remember that it is not our brother, sister, friends and relatives, or any other person who is dealing with us. It is God who is dealing with us. We have to see this. We have to realize that the Lord has been disciplining us and dealing with us all these years. Because of our ignorance we have put the blame on others or even on fate. This is total ignorance of God's hand. It is wrong. We have to remember that everything has been measured to us by our God. The amount, the length, and the intensity of what befalls us are all measured by Him. He orders everything around us, the only purpose of which is to break our conspicuous, obtuse, and hard spots. May the Lord be gracious to us and show us the meaning of His work in us. May He grant us much light to expose us and to humble us. If the Lord breaks our outer man, we will no longer present others with our strong self when we touch them. Instead, our spirit will flow out whenever we touch men.

We pray that the church will come to know God in a way as never before. We also pray that God's children will receive unprecedented blessings from God. The Lord has to adjust our being until we become proper. Not only must the gospel be proper; the gospel preacher also must be proper. Not only must the teaching be right; the teacher also must be right. The question is whether or not God will be released through our spirit. When the spirit is released, it will touch many in this world who are in need of the spirit. No work is more important or basic than this, and no other work can replace this. The Lord's attention is not on our doctrine, our teaching, or our message. He is asking what impression we are giving to others. What is coming out of us? Are we drawing others to ourselves or to the Lord? Do they touch doctrines, or do they touch the Lord through us? This is a very serious question. If this question is not resolved, all of our labor and work will not be worth much.

Brothers, the Lord cares more for what comes out of us than for what we say with our mouth. Every time we contact someone, invariably something comes out of us. Either our self comes out or God comes out. Either the outer man comes out or the spirit comes out. Brothers, let me repeat the question: "When we stand before men, what comes out of us?" This is a fundamental question that needs to be resolved. May God bless us and may we see the light.

PLIABLENESS AFTER THE BREAKING

PLIABLENESS AND THE BREAKING OF THE WILL

God uses many ways to break our outer man, and these ways vary from person to person. This is the reason the Holy Spirit directs different kinds of disciplining works to different persons. With some people, God deals specifically with their self-love. Again and again God orders environments that deal with their self-love. With other people, God deals with their pride. Again and again God orders environments that break their pride. With still others, God deals with their wisdom. He tears down their trust in their kind of walk which has its source in their own wisdom. He allows them to blunder and fail in everything they lay hold of around them. God allows them to fail again and again in order that they learn not to trust in their own wisdom, until they say, "I live not by man's wisdom but by the mercy of God." With some people, the Holy Spirit may order yet another kind of discipline; He may use the environment to shatter their subjectivity. Many people are very opinionated. They are full of ideas and methods. The Bible says, "I am Jehovah…is there anything too hard for me?" (Jer. 32:27, Darby). With some brothers, it seems that there is nothing too hard for *them*. They never find one thing which prompts them to bow down and confess their ignorance and inability. The Lord's Spirit has to deal with them through all kinds of environments; He has to strike again and again. These ones will find that in spite of their boasting about everything, they cannot accomplish anything. Things they consider to be easy turn out to be the causes of failure and embarrassment. The Holy Spirit chooses to humble them through this way. Simply put, the Spirit strikes different men at different points.

The Spirit also deals with everyone at different speeds. With some, the Lord's rod visits them in a relentless, rapid sequence. With others, the Lord deals with them for a while and then gives them a period of respite. But one thing is unchanging: He always scourges those whom He loves. We should find many bruised spots among God's children. These are the result of the work of the Holy Spirit. When chastisement comes, it may hit different spots, but the goal is the same. Whatever outward form the chastisement takes, inwardly these chastisements always wound the person himself. God may choose to deal with our self-love. He may choose to deal with our pride, our wisdom, or our subjectivity. Whatever point He touches, the result of every dealing is to make us weaker than before. He deals with us repeatedly until our self is wounded and we are weakened. Some are touched in a particular way in their emotion. Others are touched in a particular way in their mind. Whatever area a man is touched in, the end result is the breaking of the will. He may be hit in one area, but the breaking is always applied to the self and the will. We are all stubborn. Our will is stubborn. Our stubborn will is boosted by our mind, our proposals, our self-love, our emotion, and our wisdom. The things that sustain our stubborn will may be different, but in every case there is a hardness of the will. The smiting, dealing, and breaking work of the Holy Spirit may be different, but the final and intrinsic cutting work is the same—it deals with the self and strikes at the will.

Therefore, everyone who is subdued, either by revelation or by discipline, shows one characteristic—pliableness. Pliableness is a mark of a broken man. Those who are broken by God are pliable before Him. Our outward shell is hard and closed because there are many things which prop up these hard things in us. We are like a house that is supported by many pillars. These pillars keep the house from collapsing. When God removes the pillars one by one, the house collapses. Once the outward supporting structure is dismantled, the inward self collapses. We should not think that those who speak softly are free from any stubbornness in the will. We should not think that those who are subdued in their voice are pliable in their will. Many soft-spoken ones are very hard within. Hardness has to do with our nature, not with our voice. Many people seem to be outwardly milder than others; they appear to be not as quick and loud. But before God they are just as stubborn, hard, selfish, and self-confident. The supporting elements which prop up our inner structure may be different, but the inner structure is the same. The self, the will, is just as strong. The Lord has to remove these supporting elements one by one. He has to break them one by one. This is the reason He deals with us once, twice, and repeatedly. By the grace of God, something will be knocked off of us through these repeated dealings. Such a severe chastisement will produce a fear in us when we try to do the same thing again. We will know that if we do the same thing again, the Lord will smite us again. If we say the same thing again, the Lord will chastise us again. We no longer will be so free to act. It seems as if God has only touched something outward. But actually, our very being has become softened; we no longer can stand in the area in which we are touched. At least in that particular area we will not dare to disobey the Lord or insist on our ideas anymore. Out of fear of the Lord's chastisement, we no longer dare to move. We fear God, and we become mellowed in that particular area. The more we experience God's dealing, the more pliable we will become. The more God carries out the breaking work in us and the wider the scope of this breaking becomes, the quicker we will be mellowed. Pliableness is a result of breaking.

When we contact certain brothers, we can say that they are gifted, but we have the feeling that they are not yet broken. This is the condition of many people: They are gifted, but they are not broken. Others can sense this. As soon as they touch these ones, they can sense the hardness in them. Once they are broken, they become soft. If a man is never broken, he will surely remain hard. In whatever area a man experiences God's chastisement, he will be purged from boasting, pride, carelessness, and lawlessness in that same area. He will fear God with respect to that area, and he will become pliable in that area.

The Bible uses many symbols for the Holy Spirit. The Spirit is symbolized by fire as well as by water. Fire speaks of the power of the Spirit, whereas water speaks of His purity. In symbolizing the Spirit's nature, the dove is used. The Spirit's nature is a dove's nature—pliable, peaceful, and meek. It is not hard. As the Spirit of God works His nature into us step by step, we acquire a dove's nature. The pliableness that comes as a result of a godly fear is a mark of the Spirit's breaking work.

DIFFERENT MANIFESTATIONS OF PLIABLENESS

Once a man is broken by the Holy Spirit, he will manifest a pliableness that comes from a fear of God. When others contact him, they no longer will find him as hard, fierce, and severe as before. Having been dealt with by the Lord, his voice becomes subdued, and his attitude becomes softened. He begins to fear God inwardly, and this fear spontaneously flows out through his attitude and words. Spontaneously, he becomes a pliable man.

Easy to Be Dealt With

What is a pliable person? A pliable person is one who is easy to be dealt with. It is easy for him to speak to others and easy for him to ask from others. When a man is broken before God, it becomes easy even for him to make confessions and to weep. It is very hard for some people to weep. This does not mean that weeping has any merit in itself. But it does means that when a man has passed through God's dealing, his outward disposition, thoughts, emotion, and will are shattered, and it becomes easy for him to see his mistakes and to make confessions. It will not be difficult for others to talk to him. The shell in him is broken, and his emotion and mind will have the capacity to accept others' opinions and to allow others to speak to him and teach him. He will be brought into a new realm, and he will be able to receive help anytime and anywhere.

Easy to Have Feelings

A pliable man is one who has sensitive feelings. Because his outer man is broken, it is easy for his spirit to be released, and it is easy for him to touch the brothers' and sisters' spirits. As soon as their spirits move, he will sense it. His feelings become very sensitive. He immediately knows whether something is right or wrong. As soon as others' spirits move, he will respond. He will not do anything foolish or insensitive, and he will not do anything that offends others' feelings. We often carry on with things that others' spirits disapprove of. We behave this way because our outer man is not broken. Others' spirits are sensitive about what we are doing, but we have no feeling. Some brothers and sisters often offer such tiresome prayers in the meetings that others wish they would stop, yet they keep on going. The spirits of the others speak out and plead for them to stop, but they do not have any feeling in themselves. The feelings of others do not produce any response in them. This is because their outer man is not broken. If a man is broken, it is easy for his spirit to touch the spirits of others, and it is easy for him to feel what others feel. He does not act like an insensitive person who is ignorant of things that others are clear about.

Only those whose outer man is broken will know the meaning of the Body of Christ. Only they can touch the spirit of the Body, the feeling of the other members. They will no longer act or feel independently. If a man is void of feelings, he will be like an artificial limb, perhaps a mechanical arm in a body. A mechanical arm can move with the body, but it is short of one thing—feelings. Some people are members without feelings. The whole Body feels something, yet they do not feel anything. Once the outer man is broken, a man will touch the conscience and feelings of the church. His spirit will be open, and the church will easily touch his spirit and communicate its feelings to his spirit. This is a precious thing. Every time we are wrong, we will know that we are wrong. However, the breaking of the outer man does not guarantee that we no longer will be wrong. It merely provides us with a faculty that tells us when we are wrong. The brothers and sisters may realize that we are wrong without opening their mouth to point this out. Yet as soon as we touch them, we realize that we are wrong. As soon as we touch their spirit, we know whether they are for or against the matter in question. This

is a basic requirement in the Body life. Without this, there is
no possibility of having the Body life. The Body of Christ does
not arrive at a consensus through discussion and debates,
just as there is no need for discussion in our own bodies.
Every member spontaneously feels the same thing. This
common feeling is the will of the Body; it is also the will of the
Head. The will of the Head is expressed through the will of
the Body. As our outer man is broken, it will be easy for us to
be adjusted, and it will be easy for us to have the feeling of
the Body.

Easy to Receive Edification

The greatest help that we can receive does not come simply
from the correction of our mistakes. The greatest help comes
as our outer man is broken and our spirit becomes open and
free. When this happens, we will receive supply from others'
spirits. Our spirit will not only be released; it also will receive
spiritual help wherever we go. If our outer man is not broken,
it will be hard for us to receive any help from anyone. Suppose
a brother is not broken in the outer man because his mind is
too strong. When this brother comes to the meeting, it will be
hard for him to receive any edification. Unless a head-strong
person is confronted with another strong mind, he will not
receive any help from anyone. While other brothers are speaking, he will despise various thoughts, finding them too dull
and dry. Others will not be able to render him any help. He
may go on in the same way for a month, two months, a year, or
two years without receiving any help at all. He has a shell in
his mentality, and he can only receive help in the mental
realm; he cannot receive any spiritual edification. But if the
Lord steps into his situation and works on him repeatedly for
one, two, or a few years, the shell of his mentality will be
broken. He will realize the futility of his mentality. He will
become like a child, and it will be very easy for him to listen to
others. He will no longer dare despise others. When he listens
to another brother, he will no longer try to catch flaws in his
pronunciation, mistakes in his teaching, or ambiguities in
meaning. He will instead touch the speaker's spirit with his
own spirit. As soon as the Lord moves a little in the speaker

and his spirit is activated, the brother's spirit will be revived, and he will receive the edification. If a person's spirit is broken, whenever others release their spirit, he will receive edification. He does not receive edification in doctrine only— that is altogether a different matter. The more dealings a man's spirit receives from God, the more thorough will be the breaking of the outer man, and the more help he will receive. Whenever the Spirit of God moves in a brother or sister, he will receive the help. He will no longer criticize others according to his doctrines or measure others according to the letter. He will no longer pay attention to the nicety of the sermon, the eloquence of the speech, or the soundness of the interpretation. His entire attitude will change. The degree to which we can be helped by others depends on the condition of our spirit. Men often pass by us, but we cannot touch their spirit and cannot receive any edification from them because our shell is too thick.

What is edification? It is not the increase of thoughts, ideas, or doctrines. Edification is when our spirit touches God's Spirit. The Spirit of God can come out of any man. Whether in the meeting or in private fellowship, we will experience the feeding and the reviving as soon as God's Spirit is activated in others. Our spirit is like a mirror. Every time we are edified, it is as if someone has polished our spirit a little and made it shine more. The meaning of edification is nothing less than our spirit being touched by others' spirits or by the Holy Spirit. When the Holy Spirit touches our spirit through others' spirits, we receive edification. What comes out of the spirit ignites us as soon as we touch it. We are like an electric lamp that shines as soon as electricity passes through it, without regard to whether the lamp shade is red or green or whether the wires are white or black. We do not care what the "lamp shade" is like; our attention is on the release of "electricity" and the fact that we have been revived, that we have been fed before God. Thank God! If we can do this, we will become persons who can receive help easily. It is very hard for many people to receive help. If we want to help them, we have to exert much energy to pray and work on them before they will allow us to do anything. A hard person does not receive help easily. Only those who are pliable will receive help easily.

There are two entirely different approaches to edification. One way is outward, involving thoughts, doctrines, and expositions of the Scriptures. Some can claim that they have received help in this way. The other way is entirely different, involving the touching of spirit with spirit. When spirits touch, spiritual help is found. We only touch true Christianity as we touch the second way. This is true edification. If all we know is to listen to sermons, we may hear a good message today. If we happen to hear the same brother preaching on the same message the next Sunday, we will be bored and will want to leave. We think we need to listen to a message only once. As far as we are concerned, Christianity involves doctrines. We keep doctrines in our head. However, we must realize that edification has nothing to do with doctrines; it has to do with the spirit. If a brother preaches the first time with the release of his spirit, he will touch and change our entire being; we will be washed and revived. If we listen to him a second time and he releases his spirit again, we will receive help once again. The subject may be old and the doctrines may be the same, but we will receive a cleansing and washing every time his spirit is released. We have to remember that edification is a contact of spirit with spirit; it is not the increase of thoughts. Edification is an exchange between spirits. It has nothing to do with receiving some doctrines and teachings from the outer man. The best that can be said of doctrines and teachings that are not vitally linked with the spirit is that they are dead.

After our outer man is broken, it will become easy for us to receive edification; in fact, we will receive much edification. When others ask us a question, we will receive edification from their asking. When a sinner comes to us seeking the Lord, we will receive edification as we pray with him. A brother may be in gross error, and the Lord may want us to speak a strong word to him. When we touch his spirit, we will be edified once again. We can receive edification and supply from many directions. We will feel that the whole Body is supplying us. Any member, whoever he may be, can render us supply. We will always receive help, and we will become persons who are good at receiving. The whole church will become our supply. What riches we will find! We truly will be able to say that God's riches have now become the riches of the Body, and the riches of the Body have now become our riches. How different is this from the increase of thoughts and doctrines! The difference is too great.

The more help a person can receive and the broader the scope of supply he draws, the more we can say that he is a broken man. Those who hardly receive any help from anyone are not wiser than others. It only proves that their outer shell is harder than others' and that nothing can arouse them. If the Lord grants them mercy and deals with them in strong and multifarious ways, they will receive supply from the whole church. We have to check with ourselves: Can we receive help from others? If we have a hard shell around us, we will not sense the spirit even when the Holy Spirit is released through other brothers. If we are broken by God, however, we will receive help whenever others' spirits move. Even though the move may be very small, what matters is not whether the move is big or small but whether or not we have touched the spirit. As soon as we touch the spirit, we are revived and edified. Brothers and sisters, may we all realize that the breaking of the outer man has a great deal to do with receiving help and edification from God. It is the fundamental qualification for working for God.

Fellowship in the Spirit

Fellowship is not a communication of the mind with the mind or an exchange of opinions; it is the contact of spirit with spirit. When our spirit touches another brother's spirit, that contact of the spirit is fellowship. It is only as we receive mercy from the Lord to break the outer shell and to tear down the outer man that our spirit is released. Only then will we touch the spirits of the brothers and sisters, and only then will we understand the meaning of fellowship with the saints. From that point forward we will understand what the Bible means when it speaks of the fellowship of the spirit. We will realize that fellowship is a matter conducted in the spirit; it is not a fellowship of opinions. When there is fellowship in the spirit, there is prayer in one accord. Many people pray with their mind. It is hard for them to find like-minded companions, because they cannot find another mind to match their own even if they searched the whole world. Actually, fellowship is carried on in the spirit. Everyone who is regenerated and who has the Holy Spirit within him can fellowship with us. If God removes our barriers and our outer man is dismantled, our spirit will be open to all men. Our spirit will be open to receive the spirits of all the brothers; it will touch and be touched by the spirits of all the brothers. We will touch the Body of Christ. We will be the Body of Christ; our spirits will be the Body of Christ. Psalm 42:7 says, "Deep calls unto deep." The "deep" is indeed calling the "deep." The "deep" within us is calling and yearning to touch the "deep" within others, and our "deep" is calling and yearning to touch the whole church's "deep." This is the fellowship of deep with deep. It is the calling and responding between deep and deep. If our outer man is broken and our inner man released, we will touch the spirit of the church, and we will be more useful to the Lord.

NO IMITATION

The breaking of the outer man that we refer to can only be done by the Holy Spirit. Man cannot imitate this. No imitation will work. When we say that a man must be meek, we are not telling everyone to try to be meek the next day. If a person tries to do this, he eventually will find that even his manmade meekness needs to be torn down. Manmade meekness is worthless. The only meekness that will work comes from the work of the Holy Spirit. Our experience tells us that no achievement comes through us but through the Holy Spirit. Only the Holy Spirit knows our need. He orders experiences for us in our environment. He does the breaking work.

Our responsibility is to ask for a little light from God so that we will know and acknowledge His hand. We want to be humbled under the mighty hand of God to confess that whatever He does is right. We should not be a senseless mule.

Rather, we should commit ourselves to His breaking. We should accept His work. When we hand ourselves over to His mighty hand, we will see that this work should have started five or ten years ago. But nothing has been accomplished during the past five or ten years. Today we should commit ourselves into His hand and say, "Lord, I have been a blind man. I did not know where You were leading me from and where You were leading me to. But now I know that You want to break me, and I offer myself to You." Perhaps the fruitlessness of the past five or ten years will end today, and we can become fruitful. The Lord will demolish many things in us which we previously were not aware of. Once these things are demolished, we will no longer be proud, self-loving, or self-exalting. This demolition will free and liberate our spirit and make it useful to the Lord. Then we will be able to use our spirit.

Here we have to raise two matters. First, we must know that the breaking of the outer man is a work of the Holy Spirit. There is no need for imitation by the self. But if we know that an activity is of the flesh, should we try to stop it ourselves, or should we wait for the Holy Spirit to break it? Should we wait for a great light to come and not try to put any restraint on it at all?

Our answer to the above question is: We should cease all activities of the flesh. This is different from pretension. If I have the tendency to become proud, I should deny my pride. However, I should not pretend to be humble. If I am about to lose my temper at someone, I should deny my temper. But I should not pretend to be meek. Ceasing doing something is a negative prevention, while pretending to act a certain way is a positive move. Pride is something negative, and we should deal with it. Humility is something positive, and we cannot imitate it. Suppose we are very stubborn with a harsh voice and an unbending attitude. We have to deny this harshness, but we should not pretend to be meek. We have to stop all activities and works of the flesh that we are aware of. But we should not imitate any of the positive virtues. We should offer ourselves to the Lord and say, "Lord, I will not try to imitate anything. I will look to You for Your work." If we do this, we will find God breaking us and building us up.

All outward imitations are not God's work; they are man's work. Therefore, every seeking person should learn the inward lessons, not the outward imitations. He should allow God to effect something in him. It is through this work that he will derive his outward expressions. Anything that a person does in an outward way is not genuine. All manmade structures have to be demolished. When a man puts up something false, he will not only cheat others but also cheat himself. As we give ourselves to imitations and artificiality, we will gradually be led to believe that we are what we pretend to be. Even if others point out that we do not have anything real and that we have to get rid of it, we will still wonder whether their words are true. We should never imitate anything in an outward way. It is better to be a little bit more natural in the way we conduct ourselves and allow God to build up something in us instead. We should live in a simple and unpretentious way. We should not engage in any outward imitating or copying; rather, we should look to the Lord to daily add the virtues that we need.

The second matter is that some people have some virtues in the natural realm. For example, some are naturally very meek. What is the difference between natural meekness and a meekness that comes as a result of discipline?

We should point out two things in reference to this question. First, everything natural is independent; it does not need to be joined to the spirit. Anything that comes from the discipline of the Holy Spirit is controlled by the spirit. When the spirit moves, it moves. When the spirit does not move, it does not move. Natural meekness sometimes is a hindrance to the spirit, and anything that hinders the spirit is stubborn in nature. In other words, even our natural meekness can become a kind of stubbornness. If a man is naturally meek, his meekness is independent; he is meek in himself. If the Lord wants him to stand up to say a few severe words, his natural meekness will become a hindrance to him. He will say, "Oh, I cannot do this. I have never said such a thing in my life. I must let others say such a word. I cannot say that."

In this instance his natural meekness is not subject to the control of the spirit. Anything from the natural realm is motivated by its own will. It is stubborn, and it follows its own wishes. The spirit cannot use it in any way. However, meekness that comes from brokenness is totally different; it is useful to the spirit. It offers no resistance, opposition, or opinion but is fully under the control of the spirit.

Second, a naturally meek person is meek when his will takes the lead. But when he is asked to do what he does not want to do, or when something challenges his reluctance, he is meek no longer. Therefore, all natural virtues do not lead to self-denial. All human, natural virtues can only be utilized by man to build up himself. Not just meekness, but every kind of natural virtue, is used by man to build up himself. For this reason, whenever his very self is threatened, all of his virtues disappear. As soon as we touch the innermost self of a naturally meek person, his meekness disappears. As soon as he comes across something that he is reluctant to do, his humility is gone and his meekness is gone; everything he has is gone. Virtues that result from discipline are different. These virtues are produced only to the extent that the self is broken. Whenever God destroys the self, these virtues are made manifest. The more the self is wounded, the more the man becomes meek. There is a fundamental difference between natural virtues and the fruit of the Spirit.

BE STRONG

The outer man must be broken. We cannot pretend, and we cannot replace it with anything else. We must humble ourselves under the mighty hand of God and accept His dealings. As soon as the outer man is broken, the inner man becomes strong. Nevertheless, a few people are not strong in the inner man in spite of the fact that their outer man has been broken already. But the inner man should be strong. If the inner man is not strong when the outer man is broken, we should not pray for strength. Instead, we should say, "Be strong." The Bible commands us to be strong. The wonderful thing is that when the outer man is broken, we can be strong when we want to be strong. We can be strong when we have to be strong and are determined to be strong. Try this. When we say that we will do it, it will be done. As soon as the problem of the outer man is settled, the issue of being strong is also settled. We can and will be strong whenever we want to. From that day forward, no one can stop us. We only need to say that we will do something or that we are determined to do something. A little willing and determination will bring about wonderful things. The Lord says, "Be strong." When we say that we will be strong in the Lord, we will become strong.

The outer man must be broken before the inner man can find freedom. This is the fundamental path that a servant of the Lord must learn to take.

OTHER BOOKS PUBLISHED BY
Living Stream Ministry

Titles by Witness Lee:

Abraham—Called by God	0-7363-0359-6
The Experience of Life	0-87083-417-7
The Knowledge of Life	0-87083-419-3
The Tree of Life	0-87083-300-6
The Economy of God	0-87083-415-0
The Divine Economy	0-87083-268-9
God's New Testament Economy	0-87083-199-2
The World Situation and God's Move	0-87083-092-9
Christ vs. Religion	0-87083-010-4
The All-inclusive Christ	0-87083-020-1
Gospel Outlines	0-87083-039-2
Character	0-87083-322-7
The Secret of Experiencing Christ	0-87083-227-1
The Life and Way for the Practice of the Church Life	0-87083-785-0
The Basic Revelation in the Holy Scriptures	0-87083-105-4
The Crucial Revelation of Life in the Scriptures	0-87083-372-3
The Spirit with Our Spirit	0-87083-798-2
Christ as the Reality	0-87083-047-3
The Central Line of the Divine Revelation	0-87083-960-8
The Full Knowledge of the Word of God	0-87083-289-1
Watchman Nee—A Seer of the Divine Revelation ...	0-87083-625-0

Titles by Watchman Nee:

How to Study the Bible	0-7363-0407-X
God's Overcomers	0-7363-0433-9
The New Covenant	0-7363-0088-0
The Spiritual Man 3 volumes	0-7363-0269-7
Authority and Submission	0-7363-0185-2
The Overcoming Life	1-57593-817-0
The Glorious Church	0-87083-745-1
The Prayer Ministry of the Church	0-87083-860-1
The Breaking of the Outer Man and the Release ...	1-57593-955-X
The Mystery of Christ	1-57593-954-1
The God of Abraham, Isaac, and Jacob	0-87083-932-2
The Song of Songs	0-87083-872-5
The Gospel of God 2 volumes	1-57593-953-3
The Normal Christian Church Life	0-87083-027-9
The Character of the Lord's Worker	1-57593-322-5
The Normal Christian Faith	0-87083-748-6
Watchman Nee's Testimony	0-87083-051-1

Available at
Christian bookstores, or contact Living Stream Ministry
2431 W. La Palma Ave. • Anaheim, CA 92801
1-800-549-5164 • www.livingstream.com